Hope IN THE Waiting

hope✳books collaborations

Chapter One: Help, They Hate Me!: Overcoming Personal Attacks ©2026 by Trisha K. Knight

Chapter Two: When the Heart Groans: Learning to Endure Well in the Waiting ©2026 by Sherrie Williams

Chapter Three: Choosing Life in the Waiting: Hope Anchored in the Sovereignty of God ©2026 by Sharri McGarry, M.A.

Chapter Four: Between What Was and What Might Be: Where Waiting Touches Everything ©2026 by Michelle L. Nelson

Chapter Five: In Times Of Uncertainty: Living Fully Present In The Wait ©2026 by Linda Dingeldein

Chapter Six: God is Working: In the Waiting ©2026 by Linda Berg

Chapter Seven: Grace for the Slow Healer ©2026 by Kristy Howard

Chapter Eight: The Pit ©2026 by Kim "Sparrow" Spencer

Chapter Nine: Hope in the Waiting: Finding Purpose & Joy In the Waiting ©2026 by Julie Davis

Chapter Ten: Waiting on a Dream: Your Story is Your Voice ©2026 by Amber Rose

Published by hope*books

2217 Matthews Township Pkwy

Suite D302

Matthews, NC 28105

www.hopebooks.com

hope*books is a division of hope*media

Printed in the United States of America

First edition.

Paperback ISBN: 979-8-89185-419-2

Hardcover ISBN: 979-8-89185-420-8

Ebook ISBN: 979-8-89185-421-5

Library of Congress Number: 2026938507

Table of Contents

Chapter 5

In Times Of Uncertainty: Living Fully Present In The Wait

Chapter 6

God is Working: In the Waiting

Chapter 7

Grace for the Slow Healer: 3 Questions for Waiting Seasons

Chapter 8

The Pit

Chapter 9

Hope in the Waiting: Finding Purpose & Joy In the Waiting

Chapter 10

Waiting on a Dream: Your Story is Your Voice

Foreword

By Liz Caffman

Waiting is one of the most honest—and often most difficult—places of faith. It is rarely a season we choose, yet it is a season many of us know intimately. Waiting meets us in unanswered prayers, in long stretches of uncertainty, and in the quiet space between God's promises and their fulfillment. It is there, in that in-between, that faith is tested, refined, and deepened.

Hope in the Waiting was born from that shared space.

This book is a collaboration of authors— their voices, their stories, and their sacred journeys through seasons of waiting. Each contributor comes from a different path, carrying unique experiences, questions, and longings. Yet woven through every story is a common thread: the faithfulness of God in the midst of the unknown. Together, these authors offer a collective testimony that waiting is not wasted time in the Kingdom of God.

Within these pages, you will not find rushed answers or polished clichés. Instead, you will encounter honest reflections on the process of waiting—the tension, the growth, the wrestling, and the quiet work God does when life feels paused. Scripture reminds us that "those who wait for the Lord shall renew their strength" (Isaiah

40:31), and these stories reveal how that renewal often comes slowly, gently, and profoundly through surrender and trust.

The voices in this book testify to a powerful truth: waiting is often preparation. God uses the unseen seasons to shape our character, strengthen our faith, and draw us closer to His heart. What He forms within us during the wait can be just as significant as the answer we are longing for. In sharing their stories, these authors invite you to see waiting not as a delay in your calling, but as part of it.

This collaborative work also reminds us that hope is not reserved for the moment prayers are answered. Biblical hope is a confident expectation rooted in who God is—not in how quickly circumstances change. Through these testimonies, you'll discover how hope can be found in every moment, even when timelines stretch longer than expected and clarity feels distant.

As you read, may you feel less alone in your own season of waiting. May you see pieces of your story reflected in these pages and be encouraged by the reminder that God is present and active—even when His work feels hidden. Whether you are waiting for healing, direction, restoration, provision, or the fulfillment of a promise, these stories stand as a unified declaration: God's timing is intentional, and His purposes are always at work.

Hope in the Waiting is more than a collection of stories—it is an invitation. An invitation to trust God in the in-between, to lean into His presence, and to believe that hope is not something the waiting takes from us, but something God grows within us.

Even here.
Even now.
Even while we wait.

About the Chapters

Chapter One

Trisha Knight shares a powerful testimony about overcoming personal attacks, bullying, and spiritual opposition by leaning deeply into God's presence. Through seasons of waiting, prayer, and spiritual growth, she learned that true victory comes not through retaliation but through humility, forgiveness, and guarding the heart. By inviting God to lead, remaining rooted in His love, and trusting Him to work in both her life and the life of her antagonist, she experienced deep personal transformation and strength. Her story reminds readers that even in painful confrontations, God can use the process to build endurance, faith, and hope.

Chapter Two:

Sherrie Williams shares a deeply personal story of walking through overwhelming family challenges, diagnoses, and relational pain, where her grief surfaced as wordless groaning before God. Through Scripture, she discovered that these groans were not meaningless suffering but a form of travailing prayer, where the Holy Spirit intercedes when words fail. As she immersed herself in God's Word and learned to recognize His voice, her posture shifted from striving to change her circumstances to trusting God's work within the waiting. Her journey reveals that groaning can become a sacred invitation to draw closer to God and learn to endure the waiting with faith, hope, and a transformed heart.

Chapter Three:

This chapter chronicles Sharri McGarry's journey through a life-altering juvenile diabetes diagnosis and eventual kidney failure, framing her medical struggles as a "multidimensional season of waiting." By anchoring her hope in the sovereignty of God, she describes the daily spiritual discipline of "choosing life" despite grim medical prognoses that suggested she would never have a career or children. Her narrative culminates in a miraculous double transplant and the birth of two healthy sons, illustrating that waiting is not passive endurance but a "holy ground" where faith is refined. Ultimately, she encourages readers to trust that God is active behind the scenes of their own delays, writing a story of redemption that transcends human limitations.

Chapter Four:

In this chapter, Michelle L. Nelson explores the concept of "layered waiting," where multiple life crises—such as caregiving for a parent after a stroke, job loss, and the desire for companionship—overlap and settle into the rhythms of daily life. She reframes waiting not as a passive gap between a prayer and an answer, but as "holy ground" where spiritual formation occurs and faith is refined through the quiet persistence of showing up each day. By encouraging readers to release the pressure of having life figured out and to view hope as a steady companion rather than a final destination, she affirms that God's compassion remains constant even when resolutions are delayed.

Chapter Five:

This chapter explores how seasons of waiting—often filled with uncertainty, loss, and fear—can become sacred spaces where God invites us to trust Him more deeply. Through personal stories of unexpected moves, medical fears, and a cancer diagnosis, Linda Dingeldein reveals how remembering God's past faithfulness, rehearsing His promises, and resting in His character anchor our hearts in hope. Rather than resisting difficult seasons, believers are called to live fully present in them, trusting that God is working even when His plans are unclear. In the waiting, we discover that true hope is not found in the absence of struggle, but in the presence of Christ who walks with us through it.

Chapter Six:

In this chapter, Linda Berg shares the powerful story of how God transformed her family through seasons of waiting, uncertainty, and surrender. What began as years of praying for spiritual unity in her marriage eventually led to a radical call for her family to leave their comfortable life and serve in ministry on the Mexican border, where they learned to trust God for every need. Through challenges, setbacks, and even the heartbreaking loss of her husband, she reflects on how God faithfully worked in the waiting to shape their faith and guide their path. Her story reveals that when we trust God fully rather than relying on our own understanding, He is always working behind the scenes to fulfill His purposes.

Chapter Seven:

In this chapter, Kristy Howard reflects on her long journey through anxiety, depression, and emotional healing, describing how God gently uncovered the deeper "roots" beneath her struggles. Through years of waiting and difficult growth, she learned that true healing is often slow, messy, and deeply personal rather than quick or predictable. By asking three guiding questions—about comparison, rushing the process, and choosing hope even when nothing feels better yet—she discovered that God's grace meets us in the middle of our unfinished stories. Her testimony reminds readers that even in slow seasons of healing, God is faithfully at work beneath the surface, cultivating hope and restoration.

Chapter Eight:

In this chapter, Kim "Sparrow" Spencer reflects on the painful seasons in life when we find ourselves in "the pit," facing hardship, injustice, and circumstances we cannot fix. Drawing from the story of Joseph, she reminds readers that even when life feels unfair and doors keep closing, God is still working behind the scenes to accomplish His greater purposes. Through her own unexpected challenges and God's surprising provision, she illustrates how the Lord faithfully meets us in our lowest places. Ultimately, the chapter encourages readers to trust that what the enemy intends for harm, God can transform for good, lifting us from the pit and placing our feet on solid ground.

Chapter Nine:

In this chapter, Julie Davis explores how God meets us in the often painful and unexpected seasons of waiting, transforming uncertainty into hope and joy. Through personal stories—including her divorce and the loss of long-held dreams—she illustrates how waiting is not passive, but a sacred space where God shapes character, deepens faith, and prepares us for what He has planned. Anchoring in Scripture and relying on God's presence, she demonstrates that joy is cultivated even amid trials, and that trusting Him through unanswered questions leads to restoration and renewed purpose. Ultimately, Davis emphasizes that waiting is never wasted; it is a divine opportunity to grow closer to God and experience His steadfast love.

Chapter Ten:

In this chapter, Amber Rose shares how waiting can be both a painful and transformative season, particularly when life interrupts the pursuit of dreams. Drawing from her experience of surviving an abusive marriage, she illustrates how stepping away from harm and embracing the process of healing allowed her to reclaim her voice and pursue her dream of writing. She emphasizes that waiting is not passive—it involves trust, active preparation, and perseverance, even when progress feels slow or invisible. Ultimately, Rose encourages readers to stay faithful to their dreams, take intentional steps forward, and trust that God's timing will bring their story to life.

Chapter 1

Help, They Hate Me!: Overcoming Personal Attacks

By Trisha K. Knight

I could feel the heat from her breath as she positioned herself directly in front of me, face to face, blocking me from moving. I just stood there. "Only I will be writing the words." She enunciated each word with intention and let them drop with heaviness, simultaneously glaring at me as if to say, *"I dare you"*. Still learning what it meant to behave like a Christian, I remained motionless and uncertain. This little confrontation will be filed under '*things NOT to do.'* My brain was swimming with one idea after another of what might happen. Not knowing how to physically fight, I would be the dust under someone's shoes at the end of it. For survival's sake, I learned to fight with my words. With carefully chosen words, my opponent would fall to pieces, but this was not the place for that. It no longer mattered that she was a church leader; she lost her cool. She glared at me with one of the most lethal stares I had ever encountered. Since the moment she squared off in front of me, my breath was also on lockdown. I forced myself to exhale.

To this day, I do not know what justified such a necessary response, but it lit the fuse to an explosive reaction. I know it had something to do with the script. We were only a handful of people working on the play for the church, going over the lines and our positions on stage. We had certain liberties since we were creating the play from scratch. In lieu of a calm conversation about the script, it was a full, in-your-face explosion. It is what caused me to step far back and question, *Do I really want to pursue ministry work?* I was at the beginning of my walk with Christ, and I didn't fully realize yet that leadership is just as human as the rest of us. I still believed naively that they had achieved some form of perfection. Just like letting the air out of a balloon, my view of leadership would deflate and allow me to become more gracious toward the other person, regardless of title.

At this time, I would like to address a couple of things. For the sake of ambiguity, any scenes, names, places, identities, and so on will be altered to protect their identity. We will use the terms attacker, antagonist, aggressor, and so on, to describe a person who means to cause you pain or is causing you pain. Ultimately, the names will be a description of someone who brings you down by some means of oppression.

This would begin one of the longest periods of waiting that I have ever had to endure. I was waiting for a personal change. Waiting for the other person to apologize. Waiting and hoping that my antagonist would be removed or dealt with harshly. After becoming a new Christian, everyone learns the way things really work - on God's timeline, not anyone else's. God has his own way of doing things, and it is His agenda, not ours. Waiting for the necessary growth, the inner turmoil to subside, the heart to be healed, the mind restored, a baby born, or any number of things; waiting is not easily embraced.

Fast forward ten or twenty years, and one can become very good at waiting, so that it may appear as if there is no waiting at all. Don't let this aspect lose you. There is no way around it; waiting is hard, and you don't want to miss the chance when it finally happens. It can be more difficult than working towards a goal. It is surrounded by unlimited expectations. Expectation is developed by belief. Faith is made from things hoped for that are not yet seen, while trusting in God to work it all out. Faith, when strong, can overcome any adversity if given the chance. Hoping, believing, and having faith take intentional actions. Anticipation and expectation can become unbearable when years pass, and the thing hoped for remains unrealized. Waiting with excitement and belief for future events to occur can bring forth some of the most difficult days we will live through. If one is not paying attention, the item hoped for can be missed altogether. Why must so much effort be put into the act of waiting? In the waiting, people grow, changes take place, lessons are learned, and hope becomes tangible.

Many words in relation to the Bible become action words. Waiting, faith, rest, and peace all require action on our part to bring forth the development and formation of each one. As we believe, nurture, hold strongly to, and do not waver, our waiting becomes a momentum of building, like a snowball. Layer upon layer, it will grow the smallest faith into a human-sized ball or even greater. We will develop a faith that can shake nations when action is taken. Waiting then becomes our "go word," our "movement without movement". It takes constant care and intentional attention. Active waiting is where faith is born and where it becomes contagious.

To navigate through mean-spirited attacks by another person, you must place yourself deep in the grace of God. This is accomplished by filling each day with prayers and worship to God. Worship can be done in song or musically by yourself or with a group. Worship can be an act of sacrifice, such as helping someone. It can be reached by donating time to help the elderly, teaching children or youth about Jesus, or spending time at a shelter to help the homeless. To clarify, acts of service are not a requirement but an opportunity. Placing yourself where you know you can meet God, hear what He desires you to do, and then complete the task if He has one for you. There are many ways to live in a place of worship. Find what fits you and follow through with it.

The more you spend time in the Bible, prayer, worship, or meditation on Christ, the personal attacks lose their power and purpose. For example, if you're facing a bully, you wouldn't feel the urge to run and hide. You could stand your ground and face the bully with the faith and courage growing within you. You will be able to resist the harm meant for you. I experienced this occurrence after a time of unplanned separation. I was intentionally led to be in a room away from my co-workers. They would go to meetings, out to lunch, and on training days without me. Where I sat was not on the regular path like the others. I was on a different level than all the rest, who were clumped together upstairs. When things came up, they would go without me. So, I spent my separated time singing to God. When I was faced with the actions of the others, I did not crumble; my insecurities were "set aside". I responded to the coworkers' lack in a respectful and direct way. After a time, things were mended because I was able to address the issue repeatedly with strength. So, I repeat, the more time spent with God or in acts of worship, the more you will deepen your relationship with Christ. The stronger you believe in your transformation, the easier it becomes to believe for someone else, who may be demeaning you. The person trying to bully, condemn, or ridicule you will lose their negative influence on you. It is possible to wish for a healed heart and mind for your antagonist. The more of God's love is activated, the more you can spread to others in this way. As one grows in Christ, God's voice becomes easier to hear and obey.

People who find it within their power to harm and destroy just because they can can be some of the most damaging humans. To stand strong against any onslaught of attacks, one must be covered, head to toe, in the empowerment of the Holy Spirit, so as not to lose one's mind or heart. As you navigate through difficult times and personal attacks, the following are a few basic points to stick with to facilitate change.

Invite God in to Lead You Through.

"I will instruct you and teach you in the way you should go; I will counsel you with my loving eye on you."

Psalm 32:8

When times get difficult, simply call on God to be your guide through the pain and struggles, to get to a breakthrough, freedom, and a transformation. God will continually guide you and keep you satisfied, give your bones strength, and make you an unfaltering spring of water (Isaiah 58:11). God is faithful to fulfill His promises, and the Bible is filled with them. Ask God for wisdom on how to handle the difficulties in life, and He will freely give you direction (James 1:5). It is not easy by any means when facing an oppressor who seems to want to blame you and damage you in every way. Going directly to God is your single most powerful move to make. Whatever challenges you face, God is with you.

I grew closer to God the further I lived from everyone. For a very short season when I lived in Germany, I was a two-hour train ride from everyone else doing church ministry and missionary work. It would exclude me from being able to go to events in the evenings with everyone else, because the trains didn't run at a compatible return time. Negative and rude comments about my situation were repeatedly made to me by a cruel person in the church at that time. I didn't have to retreat but stood my ground. I didn't even have to respond to that person. I learned by this time to spend extra time in prayer, worshipping God, studying the Bible, and meditating on God's greatness. In fact, all comments stopped, I eventually moved close again, and all I did was worship and pray. God did the organizing of things.

When your heart is shattered (Psalm 34:17-19), God is there. He'll fight on your behalf (Jeremiah 20:11). When it seems like there's a relentless chase after you, "your life is safe in the care of the Lord" (1 Samuel 25:29). One must be strict in obedience to God so that "everything will turn out well" (Jeremiah 42:6). God must be the shelter and protector we run to in times of strife and oppression. He is the ultimate healer.

Walk in Humility, Love, and Obedience.

"He leads the humble in doing right, teaching them his way. The LORD leads with unfailing love and faithfulness all who keep his covenant and obey his demands." Psalm 25:9-10, NLT

Humility, love, and obedience will be fortified in difficult times. When you are chased, condemned, ridiculed, demeaned, and all without retribution, God must remain the one to lift you up at the right time (1 Peter 5:6) and bring His blessings on you as you remain in humility (Matthew 5:5). God must be your refresher and guide. He must be your strength to endure so much hostility. As it states in Ephesians 3:14-20, NLT (emphasis added):

> When I think of all this, I fall to my knees and pray to the Father, the Creator of everything in heaven and on earth. I pray that from his glorious, unlimited resources, he will empower you with inner strength through his Spirit. Then Christ will make his home in your hearts as you trust in him. Your roots will grow down into God's love and keep you strong. And may you have the power to understand, as all God's people should, how wide, how long, how high, and how deep his love is. May you experience the love of Christ, though it is too great to understand fully. **Then you will be made complete**

with all the fullness of life and power that comes from God.

Now all glory to God, who is able, through his mighty power at work within us, to accomplish infinitely more than we might ask or think.

Your power, grace, and hope will build and increase while waiting for the breakthrough and transformation as you stay close to God. These are not easy times. The waiting can make the damage seem permanent or never-ending, which it is not. There is not just help for you alone, but also for your aggressor. **The aggressor can be changed when they receive God's abounding love, even when all you get from them is their fury.**

It took place over a handful of years, mean looks, accusations, hurtful comments, the kind of stuff that turned your stomach into knots and caused your voice to fail. Forget about a backbone, standing up for yourself just wasn't an option yet. The desire to disappear into nothingness grew strong at times. One evening at a prayer meeting, some snide remark was made towards me, but it didn't bother me, not like it would have before. The room became uncomfortably quiet. I did receive a few fleeting smiles from a couple of prayer participants, as if they said *I saw what you're going through, keep going, you will make it.*

Remember, in a season like this one, you will grow (Matthew 12:31-37). Changes will happen in your heart. Changes to your attacker's heart (hopefully) will take place. Many will see the love of Christ manifest through you (Matthew 5:43-48) when you don't retaliate but offer kindness to your antagonist. Patience expands. Humility is increased. Compassion abounds. Endurance grows (James 1:2-4) along with the depth of your walk with Christ.

Guard Your Heart.

"Guard your heart above all else, for it determines the course of your life."

Proverbs 4:23, NLT

One of the most important things to do is guard your heart. There will be people in your life who only bring you pain and hurt, but you don't have to stay wounded. God will help you through. Take every pain to God, every hurtful word, damaging action, every evil look, all the aggressions thrown at you, give it all to God. He is bigger and can deal with them. He will heal you and work to bring revenge or healing to your attacker. In the middle of the mess, it is sometimes very difficult to see the way through, wondering if it will ever end. God will do wild and amazing things through you because of the lessons learned in this painful season (Romans 12:14-20). Do not let offense be what derails you. Allow for God to move. Keep your eyes, heart, and mind going in the direction of forgiveness and grace. Remember, "You will be accepted if you do what is right. But if you refuse to do what is right, then watch out! Sin is crouching at the door, eager to control you. But you must subdue it and be its master" (Genesis 4:7, NLT). You don't have to overtake the attacker; that is for God. You must do your part and follow through with what God gives you to do.

A few years into my salvation, I was pulled aside and asked what God thought of my anger. I didn't respond. *What does God think about it?* I'm sure he doesn't like it when I take out my frustrations on other people or furniture. Besides, there were plenty of people around who were far worse than I. God's probably looking after them anyway. I'm one of those not too bad off sinners. Just enough not to be perfect and cleaner than many others, comparatively. It took me a while longer to understand that the inner thoughts and feelings I held against myself and others were causing me to stumble and not grow in a positive way. I don't have to protect my heart from the outside world; I need to protect it from the inside one. I need to keep a clean slate.

Remain in God's Love.

> Remain in me, and I will remain in you. For a branch cannot produce fruit if it severed from the vine, and you cannot be fruitful unless you remain in me. "Yes, I am the vine; you are the branches. Those who remain in me, and I in them, will produce much fruit. For apart from me you can do nothing.
>
> John 15:4-5, NLT

God is the ultimate power source. To gain success in any life circumstance, you must remain with God. He will direct you to the path of change and healing. He will keep you safe in all situations. When you are in the middle of God's love and position for your life, no matter what takes place, there will be a triumph at the end. God pours out hope to the hopeless and strength to the weak. He does incredible feats and overcomes the darkest adversity. He helps you to fight correctly (1 Timothy 6:12) or takes over and fights on your behalf. Your strategy of humility, standing strong against the enemy (James 4:7), will serve you best. Since you have become God's chosen vessel of love, show it well. Love each other as Christ has loved you. (John 13:34-35). Remember, sowing will bring a return; make sure it's a good seed (Luke 6:38). And finally, become that spring of water that brings life (John 4:14) to you, your family, friends, and even your enemies. Stay close to God, and though your walk may be challenging, there's no better place than under the protection of the Almighty.

Matthew 5:44 (NLT) says, "But I say, love your enemies! Pray for those who persecute you!"

God will bring you through a situation that He knows you're ready for, even when you don't believe it yet. This happened when I least expected it: a person showed up who was cruel to me in the past. I never thought I'd see him at my friend's house. I was taken by surprise. I didn't have time to practice a smart rebuttal or, at the very least, make an escape plan to avoid him at all costs. The same remarks I'd heard repeatedly back then, *"You don't listen," "You're not good enough," "Why are you here?" "People are leaving because of you,"* began repeating in my head; this time, they quickly faded. That's when I knew it was different this time around. My heart did not drop into a bottomless well of agony. He stared at me, just like before, but I did not feel the need to run. I felt stronger. I felt equipped to handle any attack he might bring this time around. I even felt a twinge of empathy towards him; I heard he recently lost his mother.

I began praising God inside my head. I was thanking God for all the growth He had done on the inside of me. If I can face this person with new inner strength, the one who was so depleting to me, then God really does do miracles. I was so energized by the change in me that I began smiling and couldn't stop it. He became curious about it. I could tell by his face that he was confused. He tried to speak to me, but I just walked away. A quote from a film kept repeating in my head, *"You have no power over me."* I no longer fret over this person or people like him. God's transforming power is alive in me. Thank you, God.

Remember, it is a daily battle, and the Lord can transform your heart if you allow Him. This gives birth to a new perspective. It could be that your transformation is not the only reason you will go through something so difficult. Hope for victory in your life and the aggressor's life. Your prayers given on behalf of the attacker may be the only open door for that person to be brought into God's salvation and transformation. It could be that the person hurting you may never change. Sometimes you must come to terms with that in your own soul and then simply move on.

One thing I've always done is search for words that support the changes I'd like to see in me. In other words, if I desire to see myself become more faithful, I will look for songs, scriptures, or sayings that echo faithfulness. I encourage you to read *Still I Rise* by Maya Angelou, which stirs up inner strength and courage.

I encourage you to find things that are appropriate for you. Create a song or poem, or just search for one in a book. The most powerful catalyst to change is God's word. Memorizing scripture can be life-changing if you take the time for it. The more you say God's word, the more you read and hear it, the stronger it grows within you. The following are just a few reminders of what we covered.

Remember to:

- Invite God in to Lead You Through.
- Walk in Humility, Love, and Obedience.
- Guard Your Heart.
- Remain in God's Love.

Find Your Own Inspirational items or habits:

Find and memorize scriptures appropriate to your situation. (Example: The scriptures in this text.)

Find and play songs suited to your situation.

Spend time in worship.

Meditate on a previous victory God brought you through.

Find an item, i.e., a cross necklace, a photo, etc., and keep it with you or in a very visible place as a physical reminder of God's faithfulness.

Read stories of victories and hope through Christ.

Pray Without Ceasing.

See that no one pays back evil for evil, but always try to do good to each other and to all people. Always be joyful. **Never stop praying.** Be thankful in all circumstances, for this is God's will for you who belong to Christ Jesus. Do not stifle the Holy Spirit.

1 Thessalonians 5:15-19, NLT (emphasis added)

Throughout your day, when your mind begins to race, give a little prayer on your own behalf. If you encounter your antagonist, pray for strength and humility for yourself. Pray for others to have forgiveness, the salvation of Christ, and their heart to be flooded with God's love and joy.

Prayer:

Lord, Please help me to call on You at every moment of need during this time. Stay close to me and guard me from making my own moves and decisions. Help me to always heed Your will. Lead me to Your path of freedom and victory. Protect and guard my mind and heart so I do not fall into offense, bitterness, or selfishness. Help me to have a heart of empathy, compassion, and grace towards those who bring me hurt and pain. Thank You for Your strength to endure and bring glory to Your name. Give me the courage to follow where You lead. Show me how to pray for the one who intentionally hurts me, so they too can have a breakthrough. Make their hearts desire and respond to You. Bless them with grace and humility. Bring your resolution of these circumstances so your glory may shine bright. Amen.

Chapter 2

When the Heart groans: Learning to Endure Well in the Waiting

By Sherrie Williams

"I SAY TO MYSELF, 'THE LORD IS MY PORTION; THEREFORE I WILL WAIT FOR HIM.' THE LORD IS GOOD TO THOSE WHOSE HOPE IS IN HIM, TO THE ONE WHO SEEKS HIM;"
LAMENTATIONS 3:24-25, NIV

I pulled at my clothes and my chest, trying to physically rip the heaviness from my body. I had never felt anguish like this. I had no words, but I could feel the lament with my whole body. A groan like no other escaped my tears. There on my kitchen floor, while my children slept, my soul screamed, "Enough is enough!"

I was begging and pleading with God to make my suffering stop, but each day seemed to bring a new hurdle I had to overcome. I was exhausted and overfunctioning to maintain a sense of normalcy. My thoughts were consumed with doctors, specialists, and books. Each claiming to give me a bit more knowledge on any one of the cards I had been dealt, each claiming to have the missing tool I needed to change the path, and each one, though insightful, ultimately letting me down. I wanted my life back. The life where alcoholism didn't cloud our story. The life where there was no ODD (Oppositional Defiance Disorder) or ASD (Autism Spectrum Disorder) or OCD (Obsessive Compulsive Disorder) or any other 3 letter diagnosis someone wanted to write next to any of our names. The life where we were a whole family growing together and serving God.

Overtaken by sadness and confusion, I turned to the only stable thing I knew: the word of God. In Psalm 22, David writes, "My God, my God, why have you forsaken me? Why are you so far from saving me, from the words of my groaning? O my God, I cry by day, but you do not answer, and by night, but I find no rest." (Psalm 22:1-2, ESV) David knew my pain, he put words to it, and I found comfort in that, but even as the morning came, the groaning did not cease. Its rumble still ached in my chest, and nothing I did would remove it. Little did I know that that night, that groan that brought me to my knees would actually become my sacred threshold.

Travailing Prayer

The Bible is full of groaning. But what we see each time is that the groan accompanies a prayer of lament. David, in Psalm 22, is lamenting why God has left him. We see it in Job 3 when Job is cursing the day of his birth. And of course, we see the groaning in Exodus as the Israelites wrestled with having their comforts taken from them to be led into the desert. Each time the groaning comes when there is despair and sadness, when it all feels lost, and when the light at the end of the tunnel can't be seen.

As I read these passages, I could relate to the groaning, and yet the groaning still felt pointless. It felt heavy and like the worst kind of suffering. That was until I began to study groaning as a whole and came across something called the travailing prayer. A travailing prayer is a prayer that comes from deep within the soul. It is a prayer that, like a mother's groans in childbirth, brings forth something new. (Isaiah 66:8 KJV). This is the groaning I experienced that night on my kitchen floor, and I would venture to guess this is the groaning you yourself have experienced. It is the groaning that escapes us as we move into the liminal space, the space between what was and what is to come. It is the space where change feels the hardest. But it is also the space where change is invited. In his book *Travail in Prayer: How Groanings in the Spirit Birth Revival, Healing, and Victory* Thiery Kampoy tells us, "Ordinary prayer is communication with God. Travail is more: it is **spiritual labor** that pushes God's promises from the unseen realm into manifestation.... It is not something we manufacture but something the Spirit ignites in us when heaven wants to release a breakthrough, revival, or destiny."

The thing about a travailing prayer is that it lacks words; it is a groan like no other. It rumbles from so deep within your soul that you can hardly stand while praying. It will quite literally bring you to your knees, everything in you collapsing so that all your strength can go into the prayer. It is here in that moment of collapse that the Holy Spirit meets us. Romans 8:26 (ESV) tells us "Likewise the

Spirit helps us in our weakness. For we do not know what to pray for as we ought, but the Spirit himself intercedes for us with groanings too deep for words."

The echo of a groan was first felt when I moved my family across state lines. My husband and I so clearly heard God call us away from our home, and so, with a kingdom yes, we grieved what we left behind and moved forward; hardly a year later, I would find myself on the floor trying to rip out the groan that had settled in my chest, as over the course of several months, we were faced with life-defining diagnoses, and my husband and I had temporarily separated. I didn't have the words to pray. Even when I tried, nothing came. I travailed in prayer on the kitchen floor, on my friend's couches, and at the altar of Jesus.

The Israelites travailed in prayer in the desert, asking to go back to Egypt. Where have you travailed in prayer? Can you relate? I know I can. On multiple occasions, I have researched moving back to the city I lived in before life happened. I thought if I could just move back, I could erase the pain I was experiencing. I knew God had called us to move, but I didn't really understand why, and all I wanted was the familiarity of what I had known to bring me comfort on the hard days. God, in his wisdom, has not opened that door to go back, and I can see now how he used the move and my longing to draw me deeper into a relationship with him.

The groaning usually comes when we feel lost and are unsure of God's plan for us. It can leave us feeling as though we don't know what we need at the moment, just that we need something. Romans 8 reminds us that the Holy Spirit intercedes on our behalf. That the Holy Spirit prays in the form of groans, in a language we can't understand, but that our spirit feels and God hears. Your travailing prayer, that groan that aches deep within you to escape, it is the Holy Spirit's prayer to God.

God's Still Small Voice

I eventually picked myself up off the floor, only to find myself there again and again. Collapsed, tears flowing, making this horrid sound I couldn't control. After some time, I would feel a wave of peace wash over me. A peace not of this world, a peace we only find in Jesus, because true peace is not found in our circumstances. It is not found in our comfort spaces or food. It is not found in the familiarity we seek. True peace is found only in Jesus (John 14:27).

Each day, each groan brought a desire for God. I wanted to put words to the conversation my soul was having with the Trinity, and so I opened my Bible like I never had before. Hebrews 4:12 reminds us that the Bible is the living word, alive and active. When we are struggling, the Bible is a tangible way to converse with God. The Bible may not have a story or words that match our exact situation, but the stories found in there, his words, actively speak to each of us and our personal story. (Hebrews 4:12).

There are a variety of ways to dive into God's word, and it may take some time to find the one that works for you. At the end of the day, it's not the method that matters; the goal is to learn what his voice sounds like and to be able to recognize it when he speaks into the waiting.

If you are a person who likes to read, a regular practice of opening God's word may be where God wants to meet you. That might mean reading through the Bible in its entirety; I started in Genesis and went through Revelation over the course of three years. Other options would be to choose a devotional or a guided reading plan. You may even consider searching in an app such as YouVersion for a reading plan that is specifically designed for your circumstances.

If your faith is more experiential, and you meet God through your experiences and feelings, pay attention to the verses or passages that come to mind throughout the day, or the ones someone shares with you or prays aloud. If a particular song moves you, write down the lyrics. When you have a moment, look at the lyrics and find the passages of scripture they reference. Read the truths and let them sink into and soothe your soul.

If you are more action-oriented, you might consider a regular practice of memorizing and proclaiming God's word. Here are two ways to do this...

1) Use a set of note cards to practice and test yourself. On one side write the verse, and on the other write the first letter of each word. Shout-out to Dwell Differently for the first letter strategy to support memorization.

2) Use a set of post-its, write the verse, and post it everywhere and anywhere you will be prone to read it. Such as on the bathroom mirror, your car steering wheel, and the kitchen cabinet next to the stove. Then, when you are brushing your teeth or cooking dinner, read it aloud over and over. Go slowly, taking in each word as it washes over you.

I personally have used each of these practices at different points. Sometimes I would hear a song that would speak to my soul, and I would write down the lyrics. Later, when I would ask God to show me the truth behind the lyrics, he would show me a verse I knew I had to memorize. Here are some of those verses...

For my thoughts are not your thoughts, neither are your ways my ways," declares the Lord. "As the heavens are higher than the earth, so are my ways higher than your ways and my thoughts than your thoughts."

Isaiah 55:8-9

And he said, "O man greatly loved, fear not, peace be with you; be strong and of good courage." And as he spoke to me, I was strengthened and said, "Let my Lord speak, for you have strengthened me.

Daniel 10:19, ESV

For I know the plans I have for you," declares the Lord, "plans to prosper you and not to harm you, plans to give you hope and a future."

Jeremiah 29:11

The Lord will fight for you; you need only to be still.

Exodus 14:14

These verses spoke to me and my longings in the waiting; when I needed to know a plan, to see a way out of suffering, they reminded me that God had a plan. They encouraged me that I was not fighting my battles alone, but that God saw me in my suffering and was working to bring the brokenness into reconciliation. These verses may not speak directly to your situation, but God will speak to you, and he will show you the verses you need.

God designed us humans in this crazy way, where when we find something we love, we will thirst for more of it, crave more of it. We often experience this when we eat sweets or interact with screens. The dopamine hit we get from those experiences leads to a desire for more. The same is true when we fall in love with His word. Victor Raj Medari, author for the Gospel Coalition, explores this role of dopamine and our spiritual formation in his article *Dopamine, Desire and Discipleship* if you'd like to read more about it.

The more time I spent in the word, the more I wanted to be in his word. With each encounter, I began to know him more and more intimately. I began to recognize his still small voice and hear it speaking to me in the quietest of moments. The word became my safe haven, the holy spirit my guide. Each verse gave me direction. Your story, your walk, will look different than mine. Your Groan, like mine, is a prayer and an invitation. It serves the sacred purpose to draw you to God and his word. Whether you meditate on a single verse or entire passages, God's word is filled with encouragement and guidance for you. When our thoughts ruminate on what we think or wish we could or should be doing, the spirit reminds us that God's way is better. When we fear the future, it reminds us that we don't need to be afraid because the Prince of Peace walks with us and gives us courage. When we fear the plan and question the path we are on, the word reminds us that God has good plans for us, He cares and provides for us just as He does the birds of the air and the fish of the sea (Matthew 6:26, ESV).

Posture Change

When the groaning began, I was lost and confused, disoriented in a space I didn't know. But as I dove into God's word and learned his voice, I began to see his fingerprints along the path. Maybe you have started to see those in your walk. Maybe the smallest seed was planted, creating curiosity in a person who wasn't curious before. Or maybe it's a glimmer of fruit, a delightful change in a behavior or circumstance. Moments of self-control, patience, or joy that you don't remember experiencing before. I prayed, asking him to open my eyes, to give me wisdom, to help me see his path. The more I allowed him to show me what he was doing, the more I began to hear his still small voice speaking into my waiting. I didn't know what my journey would hold any more than you know what yours holds, but when we walk with God, we walk in the confidence of knowing our waiting will end in joy and a God-defined restoration. We can't know if it will happen on this side of heaven. I hope it does for each of us, but at the end of the day, the conviction of knowing it to be true can carry us through the hard parts.

Having the confidence, however, doesn't make the suffering stop, and in some ways, it means new ways to suffer. Like Job, we all have friends and well-meaning people in our lives who may question our conviction and discernment. It is human nature, of course. We want proof to know whether our convictions and thoughts are true; we want evidence of the work God is doing. Yet those questions can plant seeds of doubt. No longer are we groaning because of our suffering alone, but now we are also carrying the weight of defending a truth only our souls and God know.

The problem with this extra weight is that it calls for our attention. Screams for it even. We find ourselves fixated on the search for evidence, and the only way to do that is to have our eyes diligently on the people and circumstances at the root of our suffering. We look for any tangible physical evidence that proves our conviction, becoming hyper-fixated on the exterior of ourselves, others, and our situation. I don't know about you, but when I focus on the exterior, the tangible choices and actions of myself and others, I quickly become discouraged with myself and with God.

It is not enough to allow the spirit to direct the exterior. We must also learn to let the spirit guide and change our interior. The scriptures I read gave me practical guidance for how to respond and act towards the people and situations around me. Ultimately, however, they did not stop the groaning. They alone were not enough. Why? Because God doesn't seek our actions; he seeks our hearts.

The Bible teaches us that God ultimately wants our hearts. It's not our actions or works that save us; it is our heart posture that allows us to receive and follow Jesus. This might be the hardest part of walking with God. It sounds so easy: "Just focus on God," and "Turn towards him." But let's be real here; God is real and living, and we can see his mark all over creation, but he is not tangible in the way your phone or this book is tangible. It takes faith to have a heart posture towards God. Hebrews 11 tells us faith is the assurance of things hoped for and the conviction of things not seen. (Hebrews 11:1, ESV).

Right there in his word, God gives us the road map to how to change our interior. Telling us that even when we doubt, we must carry faith, being confident in our conviction. Seems contradictory to me. Being human means we are sometimes fickle creatures. We live in a grey world where we can be both discouraged and hopeful at the same moment, and here God asks us to be both confident and hopeful in his promise while acknowledging our doubt. It doesn't make a lot of sense in our physical world that prioritizes evidence over soul knowledge, but it makes perfect sense in the light of Jesus. He is a walking contradiction, of course, being both man and God.

When I finally surrendered to this apparent contradiction, I was at my lowest point to date. I was waiting to see the wholeness he promised. My litmus test was whether or not my people were thriving in life. We were most certainly not thriving. I myself had now gone into a full nervous system breakdown. (Another diagnosis to add to the list) I was overworked and burning the candle at both ends to hold the very real aspects of life together. I was striving so hard to follow God's biblical direction. In every sense of the word, I was a doer, and I was doing. I woke up with the sun to care for my kids, I homeschooled, and managed an abundance of in-home therapies and doctor appointments. All this while working into the early morning hours. Even my reading was more of a task list than a hobby as I worked my way through every book I could about autism, parenting, and mental health. I was determined to do whatever it took to change my situation and "help" my family, and yet each day felt hopeless, and my struggle was never-ending. Do you know that feeling of thinking something you do will make the yoke light, but instead it becomes ten pounds heavier?

In the spring of 2023, that heavy yoke was unbearable, and my groaning once again took me out at the knees. I sat on a friend's couch as the night turned to morning, while they lay witness to my groaning. I told them I couldn't board the plane the next morning and return to my life. It was too much, and I needed something, anything to change. They held space and cried with me, and God heard our prayers and, in a crazy story of not one, not two, but three flights being delayed and rescheduled, God gave me a bit more time. When I finally arrived home several days later, I knew what I needed. I began the process of not looking at my circumstances as the gauge of progress, but at God himself.

God becomes our gauge when our questions and prayers move from how we can change the people to how we can wait in alignment with God. Perhaps you've experienced a similar breaking point in your waiting, a point when the waiting became so unbearable you didn't think you could move forward. That is the threshold, the moment where you can choose to succumb to the suffering and stay in the valley, or you can choose to ask God to show you the path out. In that moment, as hard as it is, we can choose to take our eyes off our circumstances and put them onto Jesus. Let us ask God to show us the fruit of his work. Ask him to point out the changes both in our behavior and our hearts. This is our work in the waiting. The part we can control and participate in.

As we seek to grow our knowledge through his word, He will draw our eyes to the things that matter to him. Giving us things to focus on outside our circumstances, things that serve him. This might look like volunteering with the church or finding other service opportunities (John 15:12). Or it might be as simple as our thoughts becoming focused on him and things that bring him joy (Philippians 4:8). As our thoughts and time fill with things that delight him and give him glory, we will experience the fruit of his spirit, most importantly joy, and where there is joy, there is hope. That subtle shift becomes a testament to our posture change. It becomes the substance that allows us to wait well.

I wish I could say it is an easy course correction, but it's not. I am still working on shifting my own heart posture. The shift requires a daily and sometimes moment-by-moment intention to seek him. A regular practice in opening his word, praying that he shows us what to focus on each day, and continued prayers asking him to use us, to give us wisdom, discernment, to remove doubts, and to affirm convictions. Each action makes the process a little easier.

The groaning may never fully go away. To this day, I can still feel the slight rumble of a groan, but it is moving from this thing that took me out at the knees to a low, constant companion. The groan is our invitation to turn towards God, the embodiment of the Holy Spirit, a physical reminder that God is with us. Let us lean into it, no longer waiting with eyes fixed on an outcome or change in circumstances, instead with eyes searching for the fruit of Jesus.

The Bible reminds us all creation groans this side of eternity, and none of us is an exception (Romans 8:22, ESV). Our groaning is not the measure of our ability to wait; it is the sacred threshold God uses to teach us how to wait. As Paul David Tripp says in his book, *Journey to the Cross*,

"We groan to one who is in us, with us, and for us, who has blessed us with life-altering promises and who will not quit working on our behalf until we have no more reason to groan."

My prayer for you as you read this is that you, too, will learn to "wait passionately for God and don't leave the path" (Psalm 37:34, MSG).

Next Steps:

This week, meditate on the passage at the start of this chapter:

> I say to myself, 'The Lord is my portion; therefore I will wait for him.' The Lord is good to those whose hope is in him, to the one who seeks him;
>
> Lamentations 3:24-25

Then choose one action step from this chapter:

- Read Scripture: Choose a reading plan or open to Genesis and begin reading through the Bible.

- Make a note of verses that come to mind or song lyrics that resonate. Look into them and meditate on the biblical truths.

- Memorize Scripture: Whether using note cards or post-its, find a passage or two that you can memorize this week and recite to yourself when the waiting feels unbearable.

As you do this, notice what happens as you take your eyes off your circumstances and place them on the things of Jesus. When the groaning comes, do you find yourself seeking God?

Chapter 3

Choosing Life in the Waiting: Hope Anchored in the Sovereignty of God

By Sharri McGarry

"...I HAVE SET BEFORE YOU LIFE AND DEATH, BLESSINGS AND
CURSES. NOW CHOOSE LIFE, SO THAT YOU AND
YOUR CHILDREN MAY LIVE..."
DEUTERONOMY 30:19-20, NKJV

As a child and teen, I loved spending time outside. Games of tag and statues, kickball in the street, swimming at a neighbor's pool, racing around the block, and spending hours in the snow making snowmen and igloos. Such were the activities of children growing up in the 1960s-70s.

Another activity common during that time was families attending church together, and our family attended every week. As a result, I came to faith in Jesus Christ at an early age. I still cannot put the feeling into words; I just knew I needed Jesus. I knew I needed forgiveness and a changed heart, and I wanted to know God.

Not long after that experience, my family began attending a different church, a much larger church where people clapped their hands while singing and praised God aloud. It was a beautiful church with wonderful people who were energetic and full of life. It was at that church that I really learned about prayer, and it was also at that church that I learned about people being healed of sicknesses in modern times...not just in ancient Bible times. I was introduced to the concept of God's sovereignty and embraced the fact that He loves and cares about all his creation. Little did I know God was preparing me for a multidimensional season of waiting that would soon come.

Life Can Change Without Warning

My teen years reinforced my confidence as an athlete...running, skating, skiing, softball, track, basketball, and volleyball were more than just hobbies. I thrived on competition and loved being outdoors. Being strong and healthy felt natural. But at thirteen, my life took an unexpected turn.

It was a cold February morning as I crossed a major road on my way to school. A car slid on ice, ran a red light, and struck my right side. The pain in my thigh was excruciating, but I was determined. I gathered my books, picked up my volleyball uniform from the pavement, assured the driver that I was fine, and continued the mile-long walk to school with my friends. Nothing, not even being hit by a car, was going to keep me from playing volleyball for our school that afternoon.

As my first-hour class progressed, my leg became very bruised and swollen, but I had made up my mind not to complain. Then came a call from an overhead speaker. The man who had been driving the car came to the school and insisted I go to the hospital for a check-up. He described my ski jacket to the office staff, recalling several patches on the sleeves. My counselor in the office recognized the description and called me out of my class. Furious, I made my way to the office, knowing my parents would not allow me to play in the volleyball game after a trip to the hospital.

The emergency room visit revealed extensive bruising and a deep muscle injury, but no broken bones. Yet something had happened. That entire day and night, I felt like I was freezing and found it difficult to clear my mind of the experience. Life had introduced me, without warning, to the reality of how things could change in an instant. I was thankful to attend my older brother's basketball game that night...something that felt normal and safe.

I didn't know it then, but that accident marked the beginning of a very long journey—one that would teach me the cost and courage of choosing life and hope in seasons of waiting.

From February to June, I stayed active—volleyball, turned into track and softball—and I continued to run and exercise. But my body began changing in ways I didn't understand. I was constantly thirsty and had to urinate frequently. I learned to sprint the mile to and from school, knowing I would soon need to use a bathroom. Eventually, I began stopping at a store halfway, holding back tears and praying for strength as I pushed through the exhaustion.

At school, I became creative with excuses, asking for hall passes and slipping out of classes early to fit in a visit to the restroom before my next class. I had always been a straight-A student, trusted by my teachers, but some began to question my excuses. My grades faltered, but I felt helpless to do anything about it.

A routine dental appointment in June saved my life. Our family dentist recognized the smell of ketones on my breath and sent us directly to the hospital. I collapsed in the emergency room, nearly dying from diabetic ketoacidosis. There was no history of juvenile diabetes in our immediate family, and we were not aware of the classic symptoms I had been exhibiting.

Throughout my health journey, God revealed three things to me about hope in the waiting.

Choosing Life and Hope Are Daily Spiritual Decisions

Being diagnosed with juvenile diabetes in 1977 was a life-altering blow. I was immediately thrown into a world of frequent medical care, insulin shots, and an extremely strict diet with no sugar. There were no home glucose meters until 1981, so there was no objective way to evaluate for low glucose levels. As an athlete, hypoglycemia became my greatest danger. On more than one occasion, my parents had to call paramedics because my blood sugar had dropped dangerously low during the night, leaving me unconscious. Once, our family cat alerted my parents, quite literally saving my life.

The faith I developed when I was younger would be tested profoundly after my diabetes diagnosis. Juvenile diabetes in the 1970s carried grim predictions—blindness, amputations, and a shortened life expectancy. I heard those warnings not only from medical professionals, but from well-meaning people who believed they were being helpful.

A relative from out of town, whom I barely knew, visited our home soon after I was released from the hospital. He invited me to go for a walk and then proceeded to tell me I would likely be blind by thirty and that the amputation of a foot or leg was a good possibility. I felt defiant yet took his words to heart. I had heard prayer requests at our church for a young woman who had experienced numerous complications, so I knew he was not making anything up.

Satan is relentless in seasons of waiting. He whispers lies, magnifies uncertainty, and tempts us to believe that God has forgotten us. Spiritual warfare became very real to me—not dramatic, but subtle and persistent. Fear became a common temptation, and I sometimes found myself wondering about things such as:

- Will I live to see the year 2000?

- Will anyone love me, knowing my future is uncertain?

- Will I ever be a mom?

- Will I be able to support myself financially?

But God is faithful, and Deuteronomy 30:19-20 (NKJV) became a lifeline, "I have set before you life and death, blessings and curses. Now choose life..." Choosing life was not a one-time decision. It was daily. Sometimes hourly. Sometimes, moment by moment.

- I chose life when insulin injections multiplied into the many thousands.

- I chose life when hypoglycemia struck, leaving me feeling exhausted afterward.

- I chose life when my future felt terrifyingly uncertain.

Choosing life did not mean denying reality. It meant refusing to let fear have the final word.

Yes, juvenile diabetes was like being sentenced to an early death back in the 1970s, but I believed I would one day be healed. As a young teen, I had no idea how that could or would happen, but I honestly believed God would do it.

That was my first extended season of waiting. I didn't know the language for it then, but I would come to understand it deeply: waiting for healing, waiting for answers, waiting to know if my life would be cut short. I learned that seasons of waiting have a way of stripping us bare. They confront us with questions we would rather avoid and force us to decide what we genuinely believe about God's character:

- Is He faithful when prayers seem unanswered?

- Is He good when healing does not come quickly?

- Is He still present when life feels suspended between promise and fulfillment?

Waiting began to shape me—not as passive endurance, but as an internal battleground where hope and fear fought daily for dominance. And it was there, in that tension, that God began to strengthen my faith in a whole new dimension. It forced a question I would face repeatedly:

Would I choose life and hope—even when life came wrapped in suffering?

If you are waiting right now, this choice still stands before you. You may not control the diagnosis, the delay, or the unanswered prayer—but you *can* choose how you respond. Choosing life means anchoring yourself in God's truth rather than your fears.

God's Sovereignty Sustains Hope in the Waiting

Choosing to believe in God's sovereignty has been the cornerstone of my strength and hope while waiting. Belief in the sovereignty of God contributes to choosing life over death. It anchors our existence in purpose rather than randomness. It assures us that our lives, joy, suffering, and waiting are part of a far greater story than we can see from where we stand. This belief encourages us to endure suffering with hope and to trust in God's goodness even when His ways remain mysterious.

When Dreams Are Pronounced Dead

At seventeen, I received another devastating blow. During a routine appointment, my doctor asked what I wanted to pursue after high school. I told him of my plans to study medicine and of my desire to get married and have children. The doctor looked directly into my eyes and said my body would never be able to keep up with the demands of a graduate school program of any type, and that I would never have children. He told me I should make other plans. Despite these devastating predictions, I clung to my faith. I chose not to believe my doctor's harsh words, pushing them as far away from my thoughts as possible and not telling a soul. I clung to the belief that God had a plan for my life, a plan that included the fulfillment of my desire for children.

My high school and college years were remarkably happy and healthy. Despite the daily disciplines of a life with diabetes, I lived a life full of family, friends, and activities. I attended church with my friends, competed in numerous sports, went on a mission trip to rural Mexico, worked as a clinic specialist for orthopaedic surgeons, and earned a graduate degree with honors. Tears filled my eyes, and joy filled my heart as I walked across the stage to get my diploma, reflecting on what my doctor had said approximately ten years prior. God had allowed me to accomplish my goal and had even blessed me with a promotion at work. I was offered and accepted a position working as Assistant to the Chief of Orthopaedics in the Detroit Medical Center while also building my therapy practice as a master's level psychologist. My life was very full, and I loved everything about it! God was steadily proving that His plans were not limited by human prognosis, and I continued to believe I would one day be healed of juvenile diabetes.

In late November of 1991, I attended a racquetball/ wallyball event hosted by our church. Eager to compete, I stayed on the court during most of the event and frequently found myself on opposite sides of the net from a guy I had never met before. Bill was extremely competitive, loved Jesus, and made me laugh. The night we met, I went home and wrote in my journal that I had just met the man I may one day marry. Our friendship grew, and we saw each other frequently while attending activities with mutual friends. Then, in the fall of 1992, I had a severe case of a flu virus, and soon after, my kidney function showed signs of declining. I told Bill about the development and tried to convince him that we should spend less time together. But Bill remained steadfast. He assured me that he would be a friend no matter what the future may hold. I recovered from the virus quickly and got back to work, along with running, playing volleyball and tennis. I was feeling strong and healthy, and in February of 1993, Bill and I began to date.

One week later, I almost died.

Bill and I attended church on a Sunday morning, and in the middle of the service, I began to feel unusually weak. I felt as though the room was beginning to spin and that I might pass out, something very foreign to me. I whispered to Bill that I believed I should go to the hospital, and he agreed to drive. On the way there, I fought to keep my eyes open, feeling that if they closed, they might never open again. Upon arrival at the hospital, I was whisked away to a room, where I passed out. I awakened to nurses working valiantly to draw blood, evaluate my heart, and get me to talk. I had no energy to answer their questions. The test results showed that my hemoglobin level had dropped to four, which was deadly, so blood transfusions were immediately ordered and given. I had unknowingly been in kidney failure for quite some time, but had pushed through the fatigue to work and stay active.

Once the initial crisis passed, I was transferred to a regular room, and a nephrologist (kidney doctor) I had met previously came to see me. He walked into the room, sat on the foot of my bed, took a popsicle off my tray, and began eating it. Then he said, "Hi, how are you feeling?" During that visit, I decided I could trust that doctor and that he would remain my physician. It was the beginning of a decades-long professional doctor-patient friendship, one that would face life-and-death situations on numerous occasions.

Shortly after that hospitalization, at the advice of my nephrologist, I traveled with my mom and a family friend to the University of Wisconsin to be evaluated for an experimental combined kidney/pancreas transplant. Only a handful of transplant centers were performing the procedure with positive results, so the criteria for being on the waiting list were extremely strict. Having just recovered from pneumonia, I was quite concerned about the required treadmill stress test. My mom and our friend prayed, and I could feel God's presence with me as I walked and then ran on the treadmill. I passed all the screenings and was placed on the waiting list in Wisconsin.

Believing in the sovereignty of God means trusting that He is in control in every situation and that He can choose people and methods to bring His will to pass. We may not have a clear understanding of our next steps, but we trust that He will make our path clear when we need to see it.

The Emotional Turmoil of Waiting

The emotional impact of waiting for a transplant was profound and multifaceted. Knowing that another person must die for me to live was a source of deep sorrow and conflict. I shed many tears and prayed continually for the unknown donor and their family, grieving for their impending loss even as I hoped for my own healing. I prayed for grace and strength as I struggled to work through the tension of holding sorrow and hope together. I chose to trust that God was present in both. This experience taught me that waiting can be holy ground, a time and place to seek God until we are sure we have given our lives to Him completely.

On August 9, 1993, I received a call from the transplant center at the University of Wisconsin Hospital. It was a moment of profound mixed emotions. Gratitude, relief, dread of what my body was about to go through, and deep sorrow for the donor family filled my heart and mind as my family and I drove to a waiting jet.

Undergoing the lengthy and delicate surgery early the next morning was a leap of faith, trusting it was part of God's plan for me. Working for a group of surgeons, I was intimately aware of the potential complications associated with surgery. As the transplant team wheeled me into the operating room, I was blessed to have the assurance that I would wake up in heaven if anything went wrong.

When I woke up after surgery on August 10, 1993, everything had changed. The surgery had been long and complex, but successful. The kidney began functioning immediately. The transplanted pancreas now regulated my blood sugar naturally, and for the first time since I was thirteen years old, I was no longer a diabetic.

It is difficult to put into words what that realization felt like. There was awe. Gratitude. Relief. And an overwhelming sense of humility. God had answered my prayer for healing--but not in the way I had envisioned for so many years. Healing came not through instantaneous physical restoration, but through a long road of waiting, surrender, trust, and hope.

As I recovered, surrounded by the prayers of my family, friends, and church community, I was acutely aware that my healing was built on another family's devastating loss. That truth never left me. It softened my joy with reverence. It grounded my gratitude in compassion. Waiting had taught me that hope is not shallow optimism. It is a sacred trust in God alone.

Believing in the sovereignty of God does not erase pain—but it gives pain meaning. It allows us to trust that even delays and detours are held in His hands. If you are waiting today, please hear this clearly: God's silence does not mean His absence. Sovereignty means He is still working—even when you cannot yet see the outcome.

The Decisions We Make in Times of Waiting Ripple Outward

A few months after my transplant, I was given the extraordinary opportunity to meet my organ donor's parents on *The Phil Donahue Show*. My donor's father had received a heart transplant previously, so their family had the unique experience of both receiving and giving the "Gift of Life." It was an emotional experience, filled with tears, appreciation, and a deep sense of connection. Their son's death had contributed to the extension of my life. A bond had been established, and the parents of my donor attended my wedding with Bill the following May. Their presence, along with that of all my family and friends, was a precious gift. Love had come full circle--from loss to life, from sorrow to celebration.

Hope, I learned, is often born at the intersection of grief and grace, especially following a lengthy period of waiting.

Marriage, Waiting, and the Promise of Motherhood

When Bill and I married, we stepped into our future with joy and with gratitude. We knew our life together would not be easy, but we also knew that God had been faithful in every season leading up to that moment. After the transplant surgery, I was told that I must wait at least two-and-a-half years before becoming pregnant. The combined transplant was considered experimental at that time, and any pregnancy would be considered high-risk. Still, all my doctors were optimistic that Bill and I would be able to eventually have children.

Years earlier, I had been told unequivocally that I would never be able to carry a child. But God had never removed that desire from my heart. Instead, He had taught me how to wait without letting hope die. Three-and-a-half years into our marriage, the impossible happened. I became a mother. The joy was overwhelming—not just for us, but for the medical community that had followed my journey. I carried our son to full term, and he was born healthy and strong. According to the National Transplant Registry, he was the first baby born to a kidney/pancreas transplant recipient in Michigan, and the first nationwide to be born full-term.

God had authored a story no one could have predicted, and Deuteronomy 30:19 (NKJV) echoed loudly in my heart: "Now choose life, so that you and your children may live."

In 1999, I experienced a pain that millions of women know all too well—a miscarriage.

I was still in the first trimester but had already bonded deeply with that little life within me. Dreams had already formed. Names had already been whispered in prayer. "Why God, why?" became my cry for months. Waiting returned--not as anticipation, but as grief. It is times like that when *"choosing life"* and trusting God can be difficult, but no less crucial. I still get teary-eyed thinking about it. I choose to believe our child is with Jesus and that we can look forward to a glorious reunion one day. That belief does not erase the pain, but it anchors it in eternity. Hope, I learned again, does not mean we escape loss. It means loss does not have the final word.

Not stopping at one miracle, God soon blessed us with a second healthy son. This, too, was a testament of God's sovereignty and divine plan. Both of our sons were included in the National Transplant Pregnancy Registry, marking significant milestones in medical history and underscoring the miracles that God's intervention can bring. But more important than statistics are the lives themselves. Our sons are healthy, strong, compassionate young men. They have developed their musical and academic gifts, touching thousands of lives through their dedication and character. They are living testimonies of God's faithfulness, and their existence has already been a beacon of hope, illustrating that God's plans are far greater than our human understanding. They continue the heritage of two families joined by marriage and the memory of a family that selflessly donated the gift of life.

The Generational Power of Choosing Life

The decisions we make in seasons of waiting extend beyond our individual lives. They affect our children, our communities, and generations that are yet unborn. When we choose life—when we choose to trust God even though the path is unclear—we participate in a story far larger than ourselves.

My parents, both raised in broken families marked by dysfunction and destruction, made intentional choices to pursue Godly priorities. Their commitment to prayer, obedience, and faithfulness created a spiritual inheritance that shaped my brother and me. That inheritance carried both of us through life-threatening diseases, through waiting, through grief, and through miracles.

I wish I could say that life has been smooth and that times of waiting have been few since the transplant and miracle of becoming a mother, but that is not the case. My immune system is compromised because of taking anti-rejection medications to prevent rejection of my transplanted organs. This leaves me vulnerable to infections, and I have been hospitalized many times for kidney infections and dehydration. On one occasion, my body temperature rose to 107 degrees Fahrenheit and remained dangerously high, a level capable of causing brain damage and death. On another occasion, while undergoing a CT scan, I suffered an allergic reaction to intravenous Dilaudid, and my heart stopped.

Twice, my car has been rear-ended while stopped at a red light, and I was in an elevator that broke and dropped a couple of floors, leading to multiple surgeries, rounds of physical therapy, and near-constant back pain. Life can be difficult—even after miracles!

And yet, through it all, I still believe in the sovereignty of God.

Believing in God's sovereignty does not mean denying pain or pretending suffering does not exist. It means trusting that suffering is not meaningless. It means believing that even the chapters we would never choose are still being written by a faithful Author.

Choosing Life in Every Season

Waiting is not wasted time. It is often the place where faith is refined, where hope is purified, and where our trust in God's character deepens beyond our circumstances.

Choosing life does not mean pretending everything is fine. It means believing that God is still good. It means trusting that He is at work behind the scenes—writing a story of redemption that will one day make sense, even if it does not today.

The Word of God is truth and life. My journey through illness, waiting, transplantation, motherhood, loss, and ongoing trials testifies to God's faithfulness. Deuteronomy 30:19-20 is not just a Bible passage—it is a daily call to choose life, trust God, and hold fast to hope.

As you navigate your season of waiting, choose life— not only physical life, but the abundant life found in a relationship with our sovereign Creator and the saving work of His Son, Jesus Christ. God is faithful. God is present. Hope anchored in Him will not disappoint.

Next Steps: Choose Life Today

Today, take one intentional step:

- Bring your honest prayers—questions, fears, and longings—to God.

- Ask Him to meet you in your waiting, not just at its end.

- Commit to trusting that He is at work behind the scenes, even when you cannot yet see the results.

- Write down the promise you are waiting for, speak it aloud, and return to it when doubt creeps in.

God still sets before us life and death.

And by His grace, we can still choose life.

Chapter 4

Between What Was and What Might Be: Where Waiting Touches Everything

By Michelle L. Nelson

Some seasons of waiting come quietly. Others announce themselves in the challenging seasons of loss, change, and grief. But there are seasons waiting when we find ourselves waiting on multiple resolutions. They stack. They layer. They settle in the corners of your common hours until you wake one morning and realize you aren't just waiting on one thing. You are waiting for many.

I never hoped to carry the responsibility of loving a father who may not always remember my name, but still needs my presence. I quite literally woke up one day and found myself a caretaker. The night before, I was at a concert dancing the night away, and the next day, my mother and I were rushing to the hospital because my father had a stroke on the way to work. Everything changed overnight. I moved into the hospital with him and entered a whole new world of traumatic brain injuries, various types of rehab (who knew there were so many?), insurance, and Medicare. It was a foreign world, and I was only at the border. We weren't even at the point of dementia, Alzheimer's, or Parkinson's

Ten years later, I can honestly say I'm not the same person I used to be. Assuming the caregiver role changes you from the inside out–some for the good, and some not so much. There's a newfound anxiety that runs in the background of your life 24 hours a day because you're always waiting for something to happen. Will they have some catastrophic fall, try to leave the house, accidentally overdose on medicine, or any other myriad of worst-case, yet very possible scenarios? Your life is no longer your own. Your loved one becomes the sun because every single thing in your life revolves around their care. At this stage in my life, I never thought I'd be here. I never dreamed my days would be spent caregiving, watching my father slowly lose pieces of himself. I never conceived I would be living with my parents at 45, or that personal care, meal preparation, medication schedules, and constant monitoring would punctuate my workdays.

Coupled with this is another type of waiting–waiting for companionship, marriage, and a love story that feels steady, safe, and right. My dating life had become disappointing and toxic rather than hopeful. Each pursuit left in its trail unheard questions and unnamed wounds. Over time, hope quieted. I found myself asking God whether this was a desire I needed to release, and wondering whether it ever would be.

And then, like the ground beneath my feet needed one more shift, I lost my job. The steadiness I had in my days was stripped from beneath my feet in an instant. The questions grew louder. *How will I provide? What is next? How long will this season be?* That familiar feeling of anxiety began to creep back into places it confidently ruled before. The waiting spread again.

No one talks about how waiting doesn't happen in isolation. It overlaps. It follows me into prayer, into conversations, into late nights and early mornings when my mind refuses to rest. I often find myself approaching God with questions that don't have quick answers. Questions about timing, provision, purpose, and whether I'm behind or forgotten.

This is what waiting in the in-between looks like for so many of us. It's nothing dramatic. It's felt within the quiet, waking each day and attending to the next faithful task, while carrying hopes that remain unanswered. It's trusting God even when you feel tired. It is loving deeply while grieving what has yet to come to pass.

There are times I wish I could fast-forward through this season of waiting because it feels less like endurance and more like spiritual formation. Faith feels quieter than I thought it would. But even here, I'm learning that waiting doesn't mean God is absent. It doesn't mean He has turned away. The Word tells us the Lord does not cast you off forever, and He does not withhold His compassion, and He does not willingly bring grief. Knowing this doesn't erase the waiting, but it steadies me in it.

I'm learning that my hope in the waiting doesn't necessarily look like confidence or even certainty. Sometimes it's showing up. It's continuing to pray when the prayers sound the same, choosing trust on the days clarity feels far away, and staying in it.

Waiting is often described as a short season between a prayer and an answer, yet for many of us, it's not short at all. In fact, it spans years. It involves relationships, work, family, and identity all at once. It's not one moment in life, but rather its backdrop.

When waiting piles up like this, it can slowly change how we see ourselves and how we relate to God. We may begin to wonder if we are not strong enough, if we are not doing it right. Is there a step we've missed, a misunderstanding of God's will, and have we fallen behind a timeline that was never our own? The longer the wait, the heavier the questions can weigh.

Scripture doesn't flinch at this kind of waiting. The book of Lamentations was born from ruins and loss, and from countless days and nights spent with a broken heart (Lamentations 1:1-2). There's nothing quick about its pages. They linger long enough to name the grief. But right there in the middle of sorrow, we catch a steadying reminder: the Lord will not cast off forever. God's compassion is not extinguished by our pain, and His love does not waver because answers haven't come. The waiting may be real, but so is His faithfulness.

For us who live in the gap, suspended between what was and what we hoped would be, waiting can feel deeply personal. It is not only about what hasn't happened yet, but also about the quiet grief that comes from unmet expectations, about making the next right decision, and about gathering the courage every day just to continue on. There is space for all of that here, and we'll take a deep breath, look back, and consider how we can practice waiting, not as wasted time, but as holy ground.

Remember that Waiting Touches More than One Area

When a waiting season decides to make itself at home, it rarely stays neat and tidy. It doesn't only dwell in tension, tucked into one corner of life while everything else ticks along in allotted time. It tends to overflow. It touches relationships, responsibilities, finances, health, and more. The requests spill over. A singular little prayer develops into a quiet thread of related questions, and they color how I walk through the rest of my day.

Layered waiting carries a particular kind of weight. It is the exhaustion of holding hope in one hand while managing responsibility in the other. It is the emotional strain of showing up faithfully in visible and invisible ways while privately wondering how much longer this season will last. Over time, the accumulation of waiting can make even small decisions feel heavy and ordinary joys harder to access.

Scripture knows this, too. The waiting of most of God's people, throughout the whole of His kingdom, isn't simple and neatly wrapped in a bow. Hannah held on for a child but bore the double hurts of barrenness and misunderstanding (1 Samuel 1:5-6). David held on for kingship while facing exile and danger (2 Samuel 15:13-14). They were knee-deep in the human experiences.

I've had some staggering experiences of God's presence, but I have also felt my way through layered waiting. In times like these, I am liable to start piling it on and convincing myself it's my fault somehow, that the stops tell of my lack of worth, faith, or obedience. Thinking if I were just doing something differently, if I prayed a little more or trusted more fully, surely life would look different by now.

There is a grief in layered waiting that deserves acknowledgment. Not all losses come with clear endings. Some are ongoing, unfolding slowly over time. Dreams may need to be held more gently. Expectations may need to be released and reimagined. This grief does not mean hope is gone. It means hope is learning to coexist with reality.

God meets us here, in the accumulation of unanswered prayers and daily faithfulness. He is not only present at the moment of breakthrough, but in the long stretches where life feels suspended. Waiting that touches every area of life does not disqualify us from purpose or joy. It invites us into a deeper trust, one rooted not in outcomes but in the steady compassion of a God who remains near. Layered waiting is not a sign of lack, but a sign of refinements taking place, not for lack of presence, but for profound and faithful presence.

Release the Pressure to Have Life Figured Out

One of the quiet burdens of long waiting is the pressure to make sense of it. When life doesn't turn out as planned, and hopes run heavy, questions come fast and fierce. What am I doing wrong? Should I have done something differently? Why does it seem easier for everyone else? Over time, waiting can feel like something we should be able to explain or answer.

Many of us wrestle with the urge to compare. We find ourselves measuring out the chapters of our lives against timelines we have never agreed to but feel somehow responsible for keeping. Career milestones. Marriage. Family. Stability. Purpose. When our stories are not written according to those markers, we feel the weight of it. Apparently, we are behind schedule or missing something critically important. The longer we wrestle with waiting, the stronger the temptation to justify where we are.

Scripture invites us to something different. Proverbs calls us to trust in the Lord with all our heart, and not lean on our own understanding (Proverbs 3:5). Not to stop thinking or planning, but simply to acknowledge the limits of our understanding. Waiting often exposes that limit in difficult ways. It reminds us that we don't get to see how the whole thing fits together, and that our faith doesn't need to demand an explanation for the next step beforehand.

Releasing the pressure to give definition to all of life is not the same as abandoning hope or responsibility. This is surrender—choosing to trust God with the parts of our story that remain unexplainable and acknowledging we don't need to know just how everything will resolve in order to believe God is faithful. This kind of trust does not come passively. It is practiced daily.

Jesus addressed this with his disciples when he told them not to worry about tomorrow. Each day has enough trouble of its own (Matthew 6:34). In times of layered waiting, it becomes particularly essential because when we feel the weight of every potential tomorrow at once, the present can turn heavy. Releasing a need to understand everything all at once allows us to be faithful where we are, rather than frozen by what we cannot control.

There is freedom in knowing we don't have to arrive at clarity before we're loved or called by God. His presence is not bound by our ability to articulate plans. His compassion is never contingent upon our attaining a certain level of understanding. The pressure to have life figured out often comes from fear rather than God. Scripture invites us repeatedly to trust not because life is predictable, but because God is good.

In waiting seasons, surrender takes the form of resisting the impulse to get ahead of God. It means releasing timelines and comparisons, and letting go of judgments and self-blame. It allows unanswered questions to be as they are without interpreting them as a failure. Faithfulness in this sense is less about certainty than about obedience, less about control than about trust.

Releasing the pressure to have it all figured out does not eliminate the difficulty of waiting, but it can alleviate it. It makes room for peace in seasons where our circumstances may remain unchanged. It allows hope to settle in, not in the certainty of a future, but in the comfort of a presence.

Think of Hope as a Steady Companion, Not a Finish Line

We often think of hope as the thing that will carry us over the line into rest–a feeling that the victory will come! But that hope can feel fragile during prolonged seasons of waiting. When answers are far away, and life remains unchanged, the things that have resolved in the lives of the people we know sometimes feel less certain and, honestly, riskier. But we can still hope again, even if only to believe together that hope trains us to traverse the scenes in and through those we wait.

While biblical hope may not be an immediate resolution, it is found in the character of God. Hebrews 6:19 says we have this hope as an anchor of faith for our souls. An anchor keeps us stable, holding us from drifting with the waves that are high and moving sideways. In difficult seasons of layered waiting, this kind of hope is essential as weeks turn into months, and months turn into years. This may lead to trusting God one day at a time. It sounds like still small prayers, the less the better. It feels like showing up when we don't know how it will all turn out. Hope doesn't need proof because it rests in a relationship.

Romans 8:24-25 talks about the hope that is unseen and requires patience. This patience isn't complacent inactivity. It's endurance that blooms out of trust and opening ourselves to what God is doing when we don't exactly know what He's up to. It doesn't matter so much what we have hope for anymore, but instead, who we wait with.

There's a quiet decision to be made when we realize hope is not a finish line. We no longer measure our faith by what happens, and start measuring it by presence. We notice how God stands us up rather than just the times He answers a prayer. We realize hope can sit beside grief and loss.

Waiting can press against every area of life. We have to let ourselves believe hope can be gentle enough to stay. It doesn't have to press on or push past anything. It doesn't need to be manufactured. It must be given the room to breathe and grow, sometimes in silence, rooted deeply in the truth that God's compassion does not quit.

Hope, as a steady companion, has room in it for life even while we wait. It allows us permission to feel happy when we can manage, and to feel sad when laughing sounds unholy, without feeling guilty about leaving prayers we carry far from home. Life doesn't start after the waiting is done, and God meets us here in the middle.

When hope is not the finish line, it is something we can carry. It keeps us company in waiting rather than pressing us to get beyond it. And in it, there's endurance, and also the secret joy that we are not walking alone.

Waiting rarely ends in a moment of realization that this is it! More often, the waiting quiets itself around us, and God rewrites how we live and trust Him in it. For a woman living in a multi-layered season, answers feel urgent. God's faithfulness is not dependent on the timing of our breakthrough moments. He makes good on His promises, not on the timing of our victories.

And in the in-between, faith often looks smaller than we guessed. Faith? It looks like continuing to love, serve, and hope when we can't see far into tomorrow. It looks like giving our timelines and expectations away and just taking God's hand a little further. It looks like telling Him we're disappointed, and then telling Him again, and stepping beyond disappointment. Maybe it doesn't seem so powerful, but it's steadfast and honest, and he sees it deeply.

Hope, according to Scripture, is not a reward for endurance, but a companion to carry while we wait. If you are between what was and what you hoped would be, you aren't alone. It's okay. Your waiting graciously stays noticed. Your faithfulness is treasured. God meets you here, in the middle, with His never-ending compassion and love. Right here in the waiting, He is near!

Next Steps: Making Room for Hope in the Waiting

Waiting seasons often come with little wiggle room. When the world is heavy, it is easy for even our spiritual practices to become one more thing on a to-do list. Rather than slashing through more busywork, I pray these next steps will help you make some room. Pick and choose those that feel good to you.

Sit in the Waiting

Steal five quiet minutes to think about where in your life waiting is most present right now. You might want to write it down, sit with it in your prayer time, or do nothing but hold it in your heart:

- Where do I feel most unsure or least at ease?

- What heavy expectation am I carrying?

- Where has waiting invaded the rhythm of my days?

Release the Pressure of Having Answers

Think of the unanswered question, the unresting concern. Bring it as is to God, not asking for clarity or resolution, but as a sign of your surrender.

Pray: "God, this doesn't make sense to me. It frightens me, but I will trust you to meet me in it."

Hold that prayer and sit with it without letting anything else fill the void.

Practice Hope as Presence

Take one phrase from Lamentations 3:31-33 that stands out to you and return to it as a gentle habit every day this week. Let it work through you. Remind yourself that God's compassion is steady and His love unfailing. Hope doesn't demand answers. It begins with remembering who God is. And which of us besides Him knows the end of the story?

A Breath Prayer for When Discouragement Rises

Do this when anxiety or discouragement rises:

- Inhale: Your compassion is great.

- Exhale: You are near.

Use this prayer in those moments when you have no words.

I pray these next steps help you pause long enough to make some room in your waiting. God is not asking you to rush ahead of Him or have all the pieces figured out so you can catch Him up on the facts. He is present with you, faithful and sure, waiting with you, and walking beside you.

Chapter 5

In Times Of Uncertainty: Living Fully Present In The Wait

By Linda J. Dingeldein

LET ALL THAT I AM WAIT QUIETLY BEFORE GOD, FOR MY HOPE IS IN HIM. HE ALONE IS MY ROCK AND MY SALVATION, MY FORTRESS WHERE I WILL NOT BE SHAKEN.
PSALM 62:5-6, NLT

The Waiting Room

The waiting room was larger than most, accommodating a steady stream of patients. Highly skilled healthcare professionals wove their way in and out among those who sat in small clusters, speaking in hushed tones or aimlessly scrolling on their phones.

I took in the sallow face of the woman across from me, her thin frame and brightly colored head turban, distinct markers of the treatment she was undergoing.

Averting my eyes, I sipped my complimentary coffee, entranced by what looked like a whole lot of hopelessness all in one place.

Despite the room's spaciousness, a calm, respectful silence pervaded. The steady strains of instrumental music created a quiet buffer, offering a conscious attempt to keep one's mind away from entertaining turbulent emotions.

This was my first appointment at The Cleveland Clinic's Taussig Cancer Institute.

It felt to me that the silence of the waiting room was like one long collective breath, holding on to this moment, and wishing away any negative outcome that could forever change the course of one's life.

Everyone knew that these appointments could make your life change in just one visit.

Living In The Waiting Room

I am no stranger to God's waiting rooms. It has taken me years to realize that when God calls us to enter, He is giving us a holy invitation to spend time with the Divine. It is here that God gives us a fresh opportunity to learn more of His character and experience an overflow of His grace.

Yielding to God in times of uncertainty would become a repeated theme throughout my life, and I would not be surprised if we share this in common.

So how do we navigate the waiting room? Why does it often feel like God has turned His back on us when we are living in the hardest time of our lives, and why does hope appear elusive?

Waiting room experiences take emotional capital to navigate. Whether a small child is waiting for their birthday to arrive, a teen is waiting for their driving test results, or an adult is waiting for news of an anticipated job opportunity, waiting is hard. Nobody likes to wait. Yet life presents us with ample opportunities that have us entering the waiting room.

For years, waiting triggered an impatient spirit in me like a horse rearing behind the starting gate, ready to explode, uncoiling into action at the sound of the bell. It evoked in me a deep sense of frustration, triggering anxiety and fear which seemed to hang out right below the surface of my ever-growing faith, making me even more determined to go it alone and solve my own situation.

In time, I began to see that waiting can produce good, as it brought clarity to many obscure and confusing situations. Giving me opportunities to learn patience and discover dependence on God, proactively putting feet to what I believe about God's sovereignty. Here I found myself asking God to wait with me, instead of demanding, "How long!"

Throughout my years of ministry, God has placed an array of women in my life; I have observed that when their faith collided with adversity, they often felt ill-equipped to navigate their affliction with hope. Instead of running to God for strength, they wallowed in their misery, blinded by their pain and unable to see Christ as their source of help and comfort.

Some women felt entitled. Blaming God for any difficulty that was out of their control to fix. They grew desperate when impossible situations touched their homes, health, or children, leaving them to nurse their worry, forfeiting Christ's presence, and overcome with dread.

This has left me wrestling with what to say to those who swing too easily from trusting God to the abyss of discouragement, and to those who seem so quick to turn from God's offering of peace when they desperately need it.

Why did the truth of God's Word have such a minor impact on their everyday lives, and what would help them to have hope as they entered new seasons of waiting?

Remembering God's Goodness: When Waiting Is Hard

These questions prompted me to look back and to remember my own waiting room experiences.

To my dismay, I saw that I had similar responses. It would take years of fighting fear and anxiety before I would allow God to show me my heart of unbelief, and before I would learn that God is enough for any and every aspect and season of my life.

One such experience came during a time when I felt content with my life with family, friends, and ministry. I was beginning to see my dreams for ministry come to fruition, and my heart's desire to speak to Christian women was being fulfilled. This was shattered when an unexpected request turned everything upside down!

I loved living in Mississauga, Canada, but God was calling our young family to move back to the United States.

We were content in serving the Canadian branch of our mission organization, our two kids were settled in a small Christian school, our church provided needed spiritual teaching and fellowship, my neighbor was my best friend, and I had a fruitful speaking ministry that enabled me to travel and minister to women throughout nearby communities.

Our Mission had decided to merge with another organization, which now required my husband's job to be stateside. Immediately, we felt like we were going backwards in ministry. We had always thought that Canada would be a springboard that would eventually take us overseas, but it looked like our leaders and God had other plans.

My heart was in turmoil. I wanted to be obedient to God and our leadership team, but this move did not feel providential for our future ministry. With heaviness, I packed up our newly renovated home and tried to prepare my heart for an unwanted move. I felt myself shutting down as there was no time to grieve my loss. Mechanically, I went through the motions of painful goodbyes, cancelling future speaking engagements, and preparing our children for yet another change.

Arriving in the States, my husband immediately stepped into his new role, while at home, I struggled with two young children, boxes that needed unpacking, no church community, no friends, and no ministry. Even though I was back in my own country, everything shouted "new" to me.

Depression engulfed me, the loss felt so great, and I was unable to move forward. The challenges of this move plunged me into a very dark time of waiting on God to show up. I felt like the Psalmist, as "Day and night, I have only tears for food" (Psalm 42:3, NLT).

My persistent sadness stripped me of joy, as depression has a way of clouding our minds, causing lies of despair to encroach on what is real. I knew I needed to fight these lies with the truth of God's Word. I needed hope! I wanted my joy back.

Many days, after I sent my children to school, I fell back into bed. Overwhelmed with the thought of unpacking boxes and setting up our new home. As I lay in the darkened room, the Holy Spirit reminded me that "The LORD is close to the brokenhearted; he rescues those whose spirits are crushed" (Psalm 34:18, NLT).

As I offered my crushed spirit to God, my tears of lament fell. I needed rescuing!

Though my spirit felt heavy, I began to recall ways that God had met me in previous moves. Hope surged as I began to remember numerous times that God drew near to our family and me in times of ambiguity and transition. God was with me before, and in that moment, I knew He would be with me now.

Psalm 139 reminded me that darkness and light are the same to God. Even in my profound sadness, I could not hide from God. My depression did not put God off; nor would He push me away. He could handle my pain, and in my darkness, He would become my light.

Despite my feelings of loss, day after day I clung to God's promises, and I began in earnest to pray scripture aloud into the darkness of my bedroom.

I could not tangibly see God, but as I spent hours praying scripture, rehearsing God's promises, and meditating on His Word, God was faithful to remind me that hope will split the darkness when we turn our gaze from our disappointments and, in faith, fix them on the Deliverer.

I began to glimpse the truth that the God who is able was with me. Over time, I felt the Holy Spirit lift my darkness and replace it with hope!

God reminds us to "Remember the things I have done in the past. For I alone am God! I am God, and there is none like me" (Isaiah 46:9, NLT).

Grieving my loss in this move would not come until years later, yet in darkness, I learned to look back and to remember the places in my life where I had seen God show up, and by faith, I chose to believe that He would meet me once again in my time of waiting.

God would remind me that as we "...remember his wonderful works," we will see "How gracious and merciful" our Lord is (Psalm 111:4, NLT).

Rehearsing God's Promises: When Waiting Is Long

Loss, loneliness, and depression had thrust me into a dark time of waiting, but what about you? Take a moment. Stop and consider the many situations that have pushed you into a distressing waiting posture.

Waiting holds no time limit. It may be an afternoon, a weekend, weeks, or even months that can turn into years of one exceptionally long season of waiting.

The premise of waiting is the same, regardless of the length of time. Yet as time passes and we feel no relief, or even a hint of movement towards our desired outcome, uneasiness sets in, and we often grow anxious, fearful, and discouraged.

If we were honest, the raw reality facing us leaves us confused. We find that integrating the truth of scripture with the reality of what we feel often fills our heart and mind with disparaging questions.

"If God cares about what I am facing, why is He so silent?" "Why is God taking so long to correct this situation?" "What is the purpose of so many delays and setbacks?"

Questions like these leave us feeling alone in our struggle, letting us believe that God is busy helping everyone else but us. Slowly, we allow unbelief to override the truth of God's character. And once our hurting, questioning hearts are left unchallenged by the truth of God's Word, we subtly drift from exercising faith that believes, for a false narrative that deceives.

Years ago, I found myself falling into the trap of living out of this false narrative. My annual mammogram showed a suspicious finding, which required a follow-up scan. After multiple days of not hearing the updated results, my mind immediately went to a worst-case scenario.

Usually, no news is good news. But, this time, I was certain that no news was devastating news. So much so that when I met with the specialist for a follow-up visit, I felt positive that I knew the truth about my condition. I went into my appointment fully convinced that the scan showed that I had cancer. I had recently lost my father to pancreatic cancer and a dear friend to a brain tumor; with these devastating losses in mind, I was sure that I was the next victim.

When the doctor told me that I had nothing to worry about, that the findings were benign, sadly, my response was disbelief. I was so dismayed as I drove myself home from my appointment. What should have been a joyful moment turned into an unfortunate day as I had allowed myself to live through multiple days of worry, anxiety, and paralyzing fear instead of remembering the truth of God's Word, rehearsing His promises, and claiming His peace.

As I look back, I believe that if I had rehearsed the promises of God and rested in God's character in my time of waiting, my mind would not have fallen prey to distortion.

God's Word is clear: "Let us hold tightly without wavering to the hope we affirm, for God can be trusted to keep his promise" (Hebrews 10:23, NLT).

When the truth of God's Word gets pushed aside, we miss out on what we need the most. Christ Himself! And when we rely on our feelings, they will always trick us into believing a false narrative. By not bringing God into the equation, we cannot experience hope in the waiting. Rehearsing the promises of God will never fail to comfort us and keep our hearts and minds on Christ Jesus, our source of hope.

I am thankful that years later, God gave me another opportunity to go through this same scenario. I had learned my lesson, and I am happy to say that this time I brought God and His promises into the waiting room with me.

"You will keep in perfect peace all who trust in you, all whose thoughts are fixed on you!"

Isaiah 26:3, NLT

Resting In God's Character: When Waiting Feels Out Of Our Control

I was beginning to get restless. The pit in my stomach told me I had missed lunch. I looked questioningly at the receptionist, trying to catch her eye, but she ignored my glance with her head tucked, eyes on her computer screen.

A small huff escaped as I glanced at the clock on the wall in the waiting room. As the door opened, my hope quickly deflated. A staff member hurried past me, juggling a takeout container and a fountain drink, leaving behind the scent of something Italian.

Could I have been sitting in this tiny, sterile waiting room for over three hours? What was to be a quick eye appointment was turning into an all-day affair.

What started as a subtle whisper in my direction grew louder until it was voiced directly to me. The heavy-set man next to me shifted impatiently.

"I've been here since 8:30. First appointment of the day! I missed lunch, and I'm about to miss dinner if they don't hurry up back there!" He huffed with an irritated exhale.

Quickly scanning the small waiting room, I noticed the remaining patients. Heads bobbed in agreement as a low undercurrent of angry retorts began to fill the small room.

Everything inside me wanted to agree; I, too, had been here for hours, but in that moment, I decided that no matter how long I had to wait, I needed to be a visible representation of Christ. Joining their undercurrent of waiting room rebellion would not make the time go faster.

Giving my neighbor a subtle smile, I settled deeper into my seat and picked up my book.

Moments later, the door opened, and my name was called. A hidden smile reached my heart, relieved that my time of waiting was finally over!

Maybe you, too, have grown weary in the waiting room. The clock has ticked past any reasonable time to sit with such uncertainty. You see others coming and going around you without any weighty concerns, and you become desperate for even one small sign that relief is on its way.

In your restlessness, you frantically look for ways to find reprieve. Your mind begins to race for any conceivable scenario of how you can circumvent your problem and regain control of what feels like an out-of-control, impossible situation.

When we doubt God's timing, we look for ways to shorten our waiting. We lose sight of God and begin to doubt his reliability and his love.

Our situation feels unfair, and we grow desperate to find a way of escape. We begin to look for ways to prevent any more pain from consuming our lives. We want relief. And we want it right now!

As we look inward for self-made answers, we forget to rest in God's divine perfection. We forget that He is our helper, our comforter, a peace giver, our provider, and our all-sufficient grace. He is the one who knows the best possible pathways for us to journey forward with hope.

"The Lord says, 'I will guide you along the best pathway for your life. I will advise you and watch over you.'"

Psalm 32:8, NLT

With wavering faith, we are beginning to feel alone in our wait. Blinded by doubt, we nurse our neglected, forgotten feelings and turn our emotions inward, away from our only source of hope.

"God, what is the benefit of obeying you when all I feel is pain? I thought that if I followed you, you would do more than I am experiencing right now. I am doing my best to live a godly life, so why do I have to endure all of this? Why is it taking so long to show me an effective way forward?"

The waiting room is starting to feel lonely. Our expectations have risen to the surface, and we begin to feel like, as God's children, living our lives for Christ, we should not have to live in pain, confusion, or lack. We began to feel like God is indebted to us, owing us only what seems good in our own eyes.

We are tempted to believe that since He isn't giving us what we want, He must not be worthy of our trust after all. Or since He doesn't seem to show up when we need Him to, He isn't dependable or safe to rely on.

We become like selfish children on the playground, pouting and stomping when we don't get our way.

Feeling unseen by the Almighty, we rush off to solve our problems, and just like that, we lose sight of the fact that God has promised to be with us Himself. Frustrated, we turn away from the one who knows all about waiting.

God is no stranger to pain. As scripture says, it was for "..the joy awaiting him, he endured the cross disregarding the shame" (Hebrews 12:2, NLT). He knows how to sit faithfully in the waiting room. For thirty-three years, He waited for the opportune time to reveal His glory to the world. At just the right time, He would step out of the waiting room and give Himself as a sacrifice to redeem all humankind. His waiting would become our hope in our time of waiting.

He did not try to grasp control of His situation but rather lived fully present, yielding obediently to his Father's plan. A plan that He knew was good, because His Father was good.

Living Fully Present: In Times Of Waiting

God had been prompting my heart to learn the value of living fully present. I, too, wanted to yield obediently to God's good plan. Full engagement and humble acceptance of what or whom was before me kept me practicing this principle. I often found that God was quick to give me opportunities with people who would stretch and grow me in this area.

One such opportunity came while I was attending a local women's conference. Among the myriads of women, I saw her coming at me like a bee to honey. She was zeroing in, smiling radiantly, as if I were her new best friend. She began talking in full-on sentences before she reached me, and for a split second, I had been tempted to duck down another aisle of the conference auditorium. I felt trapped in what I knew would be a long, one-sided conversation.

I greeted her with a warm smile. Her enthusiasm was contagious; yet my introverted nature and my ire at being the targeted recipient rose quickly to the surface. Inwardly, I felt myself groan. How on earth does one person have so much to say, with no regard that conversation is a two-way street, and why has she chosen me to be the one to say it to?

Instantly, the gentle whisper of the Spirit sounded in my ear. "Live fully present."

I knew immediately how I needed to respond. God has been prompting me to live from a place of complete engagement with whoever is in front of me, because they deserve my full attention. Even if they were an imposition or an interruption. I needed to sacrificially offer myself as Christ would, with a love that valued others by being fully present.

Responding to God's gentle nudge, I started to embrace her enthusiasm. Gradually, I found myself leaning in and truly listening, no longer nodding in agreement while my mind wandered elsewhere.

I had engaged people far too many times where my body was present, while my mind was not. How many times have I walked away from a conversation, never having heard the other person's heart or missing the encouragement of their joy?

I had also engaged in life situations much the same way. Trying to find ways to disengage when things didn't go the way I thought they should.

God was nudging me to see that by living fully present, I could confidently trust God's all-powerful nature in the hardest of situations. I may not have seen the evidence of his hand of mercy, but I could trust that every detail was purposefully being worked out for my good.

I could rest in God's plan, knowing that Romans 8:28 was a trustworthy promise telling me that "God causes everything to work together for the good of those who love God and are called according to his purpose for them" (Romans 8:28, NLT).

God was offering me his all-wise plan. It was like he was saying to me, "In your pain, I am your comfort. In your uncertainty, I know the way to go. When you are lonely, my presence is with you; my eyes of love will always remain on you, and I will never abandon my own."

Even in the ambiguity, instability, the hard decisions, and the long wait, God is present, and He is enough.

Faith clings to God even when nothing in our situation seems good, because we know that God Himself is good.

God was showing me that to live fully present, I needed to lay aside my fear, which was causing me to grasp for control. And to look for more of Him, my confident hope, in the obscure, overwhelming places of life.

At this time, the apostle Paul's prayer became very personal to me. "I pray that God, the source of hope, will fill you completely with joy and peace because you trust in him. Then you will overflow with confident hope through the power of the Holy Spirit" (Romans 15:13, NLT).

It was in that moment of trust, even when I couldn't see God, that I knew that he was right there holding me up. His purposes may have seemed like a mystery, but I could trust that the character of God is for me and not against me.

God says, "Don't be afraid, for I am with you. Don't be discouraged, for I am your God. I will strengthen you and help you. I will hold you up with my victorious right hand" (Isaiah 41:10, NLT).

Everything we have ever known about God says that He is with us in the wait, but what we are experiencing right now may be telling us a different story. The truth of God's Word shows us repeatedly that God is dependable and reliable, and that "nothing is too hard" for Him (Jeremiah 32:27, NLT).

When I choose not to live fully present, I forfeit God's comfort when I need it the most.

Living fully present is an accepting response to where God has placed us in this immediate moment. It means that we cling to God in this time of adversity, instead of wishing it away, knowing that God is trustworthy and in complete control. We realize that our situation does not feel good now, but we understand that all His works are for our good.

In this moment, as we see that God is in both the blessing and the struggle, we learn the value of living fully present. As we proactively choose God's promises over our worry, fear, and anxiety, we develop a spiritual awareness that God is actively involved in every detail of our lives.

By living fully present, we allow ourselves to rest in God's divine care, knowing that He will not leave us to do it alone, and what He orchestrates is for the benefit of all involved!

We become watchful. Looking for what or whom God has brought before us and offering ourselves in service for God and others. Surprisingly, as we look at the needs of others, there is a momentary reprieve from our own struggle. This offering is rather stretching for our hurting hearts, but something beautiful happens in us as we serve others in our time of adversity.

In this place of trusting God fully, we begin to see that our trials are a means for deeper spiritual growth and Christ's likeness. This difficulty is not about what makes me feel good, but about allowing God to mold me into His image.

If we can allow our hearts to draw near to God, even when it hurts, in the good and the bad, we will learn to live fully present. We will remember His goodness, rehearse His promises, and through our tears, offer a sacrifice of praise, because we know who our God is.

Adversity is hard. If we are going to accept it, rest in it, and trust that God is working on our behalf, I have found it necessary to stay immersed in God's Word. Praying scripture has kept my heart tender towards God as I wait for Him to orchestrate the details of my life during hard times. This has kept my eyes on Christ rather than my struggle.[1]

We may see no way forward in our time of waiting, and no conceivable way out, yet we can rest in the truth that God is with us, never to leave us, and will not give us more than we can handle through his strength.

> For I hold you by your right hand – I, the Lord your God.
> And I say to you, 'Don't be afraid. I am here to help you.
> Isaiah 41:13, NLT

The promises of God's Word offer our broken spirits a message of hope in hard places.

My heart was being prompted to exchange the fretful rehearsing of anxious thoughts for learning to rehearse the truths about God's supreme character. Now my thoughts were filled with his faithfulness, goodness, kindness, compassion, wisdom, and abundant blessings.

It takes believing faith to trust that God is at work even when we lack evidence that He is working on our behalf or has our best interest at heart. But God is calling us to know exactly that!

To live fully present in times of waiting, to put our hope in the unshakeable foundation of the Lord Jesus Christ. This takes courage to step out when we are unsure where our foot will land, but we can know that it is God who "goes before" us and "follows" us, and his "hand of blessing" rests upon us. (Psalm 139:5, NLT)

> So be strong and courageous! Do not be afraid and do not panic before them. For the Lord your God will personally go ahead of you. He will neither fail you nor abandon you.
>
> Deuteronomy 31:6, NLT

We can live fully present in times of waiting when we know that God is the one who knows us best and loves us most. He is the one who will give us the confidence to take that first step of faith.

He is the one who sees us, and, despite our anger or sadness, he will never turn his back on us in disgust or impatiently walk away from our struggle.

Living fully present in our times of waiting places us right where God longs for us to be. A transformative place where our understanding of God grows alongside our trust.

This has been a repeated theme for my life, evidenced in the words I wrote in my book Praying Life in The Word, as I see God whispering to me as His Beloved Daughter:

Regardless of your circumstances, will you trust me, rely on me, rest in me, and lean into me? In so doing, you will discover... That I, the LORD your God, I am your all sufficiency.[2]

We may find ourselves overcome with anguish, overwhelm, or disappointment, but when things are falling apart and nothing seems to be going the way we want, the best choice we can make is to trust God explicitly.

As I have grown in knowing who God is, I am learning to live fully present, not resistant to God but resting in his care as I sit in the waiting room, joining my broken heart with the all-wise, sovereign God of the universe.

I may be hurting, but I trust that God knows what is best for me. When I seek Him, I will find that He is faithful to meet me in my greatest need with His heart of compassion and hope.

Our hope is Christ Jesus! Often, we think hope arrives when we are in a better situation or in the absence of pain, but Christ offers us something even better. Himself! His presence. His peace.

In the lonely, long wait, where there seems to be no answers to impossible situations, I need the faithful love of God to journey with me and to be my source of strength, assurance, and confident hope for what lies ahead.

When we stop running from our problems or quit wishing them away, we glimpse that God is weaving Himself into our story, and our waiting becomes a divine opportunity, allowing our pain to have purpose, drawing us closer to know and love Master Jesus.

When we lean fully on God's promises, we transfer the weight of our worry onto Christ, and we begin to see ways that He faithfully shows up and makes Himself known in the fragile, messy, and mundane story of our lives.

What a beautiful surprise, when you realize that you can see God at work in seasons of waiting.

You may become even more amazed that your heart has grown tender towards God, and where doubt once festered, belief is sprouting. In place of a bitter spirit, a heart of gratitude has taken root, and thanksgiving is bubbling up as you consider the grace of God evident in your life.

As we boldly step out in faith, we proclaim that Christ is with us, for us, and blessing us even as we live fully present in what feels like an impossible challenge.

In taking this step of faith, we help others see a hopeful way to walk through demanding times in their own lives. As they observe us resting in and relying on God to show us the best way forward, they will marvel at how God fills us with peace.

Peace is something this world does not offer. So, it is very pronounced when people apart from Christ observe it in our lives.

By offering Himself, God is offering us hope in the waiting. He is calling us to live in the very moment that we are standing in right now, to embrace it, and to believe that He is enough for where we find ourselves at this time in our lives.

Trust in the Lord with all your heart; do not depend on your own understanding. Seek his will in all you do, and he will show you which path to take.

Proverbs 3:5-6, NLT

Whether you find yourself grieving a loss, anticipating God's answer to a prayer concern, or challenged by disappointment, we can look at our season of waiting with a hopeful heart, knowing that God is with us all along the way.

Rejoicing In Hope: In Times of Waiting

My apprehension grew as each mile took us farther from home and closer to The Cleveland Clinic. This appointment felt different to me, and deep down, I sensed a life-altering journey ahead. But now, as we sat in the Clinic's parking garage, God was urging me towards a new posture of waiting on Him. With a fresh sense of need, we paused to pray before getting out of the car.

I felt that God was inviting me to something deeper, to commit fully to His divine providence, which would be the first step of faith in what would become one of the most difficult experiences of my life. God was preparing our hearts for what was to come.

In this moment of devotion, I knew that I did not want to waste this opportunity to see God glorified. My heart spoke. "God, I don't know what to do, but my eyes are on you!"

It was then that I realized the days ahead might not be the absence of pain but an acceptance of God's good and perfect plan.

The diagnosis that came was not what we had hoped: Non-Hodgkin's B-cell Lymphoma.

There was a long journey ahead of me, and the unknowns were filled with grave uncertainty, but our parking lot prayer helped me to keep my eyes on Christ, as my refuge and strength.

I was learning that my future was safe when I left it in God's all-powerful hands. I needed to fix my eyes on Jesus because hope doesn't come in the absence of struggle, but in seeing God's character amid the adversity. I would never be satisfied with my waiting, without full reliance on God.

We can only surrender ourselves to God in difficult seasons when we understand that God's character is enough. We do this by remembering how God led us in the past, rehearsing God's promises, resting in God's goodness, and allowing our hearts to rejoice with hope.

I would need to remember these spiritual principles as I was entering an unpredictably long season of dealing with treatments, nausea, severe bone pain, hair loss, sleepless nights, and an allergic reaction to my cancer regimen, which later became a recurring nightmare.

Waiting is hard, and nobody likes it. Yet, waiting is part of the Christian walk. As we yield ourselves to God, we grow in becoming more like Jesus, and as we grow, we begin to see the importance of the waiting room to mature us into Christ's likeness. It is here that our story offers encouragement to others in their times of waiting.

And as we begin to learn to live fully present in times of uncertainty, we see that Christ is our rock-solid foundation. He is our hope in the waiting.

Lessons For Living Fully Present: In Times Of Uncertainty

Remember: Remember how God led in the past.

I remember the days of old. I ponder all your great works and think about what you have done. I lift my hands to you in prayer. I thirst for you as parched land thirsts for rain.

Psalm 143:5-6, NLT

Rehearse: Rehearse God's promises.

For I know the plans I have for you," says the Lord. "They are plans for good and not for disaster, to give you a future and a hope. In those days when you pray, I will listen. If you look for me wholeheartedly, you will find me.

Jeremiah 29:11-13, NLT

Rest: Rest in God's goodness.

Let all that I am wait quietly before God, for my hope is in him. He alone is my rock and my salvation, my fortress where I will not be shaken.

Psalm 62:5-6, NLT

Rejoice: Rejoice in hope!

We put our hope in the Lord. He is our help and our shield. In him our hearts rejoice, for we trust in his holy name. Let your unfailing love surround us, Lord, for our hope is in you alone.

Psalm 33:20-22, NLT

Revere: Revere God's Word through study and prayer.

I will study your commandments and reflect on your ways. I will delight in your decrees and not forget your word.

Psalm 119:15-16, NLT

Don't worry about anything; instead, pray about everything. Tell God what you need and thank him for all he has done.

Philippians 4:6, NLT

Revere God: Revere God through a heart of worship.

Therefore, let us offer through Jesus a continual sacrifice of praise to God, proclaiming our allegiance to his name.

Hebrews 13:15, NLT

Prayer Of Hope: For Times Of Waiting

God, I wait in hope for the Lord. You are my help and my shield. In you, my heart rejoices, for I trust in your holy name. May your unfailing love rest upon me, O Lord, even as I put my hope in you. Help me to trust in you with all my heart; to not depend on my own understanding but to seek your will in all you do, knowing that you will show me which path is best to take.

Lord, your faithful love never ends! Your mercies never cease. Great is your faithfulness; your mercies begin each morning afresh, and you, O Lord, you are my inheritance; therefore, I will hope in you. You will keep me in perfect peace because my heart trusts in you and my thoughts are fixed on you. I love you, Jesus! AMEN

Chapter 6

God is Working: In the Waiting

By Linda Berg

My husband had a midlife crisis at the age of 40 that turned our whole family's lives upside down.

Before you build mental images of what all that entailed, I need to go back to the very beginning of our life together. This life crisis....was not the usual mid-life crisis!

One day, seven-year-old Brad scrambled down the steps of the school bus upon arriving home in rural Minnesota. Running quickly inside the house to his mother, who was standing at the kitchen sink, he exclaimed, "I'm going to marry Linda Kelley when I grow up."

"That's nice, dear," his mom responded. She let a small grin slip from the corner of her mouth as the absurdity of her seven-year-old son knowing who he would marry gave her a chuckle.

Linda Kelley, that was me. I was six years old when Brad made that proclamation to his mother.

I was raised in a Christian home. My father was a minister of the gospel. During my childhood, he ministered at three locations in the Midwestern United States. Each location and each church family brought numerous blessings into my family's life.

My parents were God-loving and faithful living people. They were not just "Sunday Christians." I saw and felt the consistent lifestyle of truly loving and serving God with every fiber of their being. I was young when I knew that I loved Jesus and wanted to give my life to him. That simple young faith was nurtured by my parents and so many others from those various church families. As a teenager, I took my faith seriously and felt I had an active, living, trusting faith in God.

By design, I say with "tongue in cheek," that seven-year-old boy, Brad, and I ended up at the same Christian College. Within a year, as Brad relentlessly pursued me, I was confident I was madly head-over-heels in love with the same Brad who, at age seven, told his mother he would marry me.

All my life, I had heard these most important and precious words about life: "Don't be unequally yoked." No problem, I thought. Brad's family had been visitors at one of the churches where my dad was a preacher in our growing-up years, and my dad had studied the Bible with them. In time, the whole family came to Christ.

So, at the age of 19, when I "fell in love" with Brad, I never gave it another thought. Surely, we both loved God; we were equally yoked.

We were not married long when I realized, in many, many ways, we were not equally yoked. Our understanding, our devotion, our living out daily life honoring Christ looked very different to each of us.

Suffice it to say, I took it upon myself to try to effect the change in my husband that would make us equally yoked. Scriptures, conversations (most uncomfortable for him), trying to engage others, and praying were all efforts I made to bring cohesion to our daily living for Christ. I'm sure you can see all the flaws in this method. I eventually saw it too.

What was driven by my own perspective and understanding was a complete failure in bringing the two of us together.

Many years passed. As I grew in my own walk with Christ, I dropped all personal efforts and simply prayed. I didn't just pray for my husband; I prayed for myself, too. I relinquished control and any specific thinking of what being equally yoked would look like. I prayed for God to do whatever he needed to do so that we could be equally yoked in marriage.

In those years, we added six children to our family, five daughters and one son. Life felt content and complete. Brad was busy providing for us, working two jobs most of those years, to allow me to stay home and raise our children. As it is for most families, those are very busy years. While Brad ran a home renovation company, I was his secretary and accountant. He farmed part-time in those years, too, managing over 2500 acres for a crop farmer. We were active in our church family, not just as "attenders" but as Bible class leaders, youth group teachers, and Bible Bowl coaches. Our children were all involved in public school, band, drama and musicals, basketball, track, and football. Some of them took piano lessons from one of their grandmas who lived nearby.

This was real Christian family life! Wasn't it?

There is a scripture that I remember hearing as a child:

At Caesarea there was a man named Cornelius, a centurion of 'what was known as the Italian Cohort, a devout man who feared God with all his household, gave alms generously to the people, and prayed continually to God.

Acts 10:1-2, ESV

I knew, as a child, that I hoped to be a "devout" follower of Jesus Christ. But I often wrestled at this stage of life with feeling "we" were sometimes more focused on "doing" than "being" what I thought a really devout follower of Jesus Christ looked like.

I continued to pray for us as individuals, as a couple, and as a family. At this stage of life, when I asked Brad if we could pray regularly as a couple, he said he felt more comfortable praying on his own. He felt, at that time, prayer was meant to be one-on-one with God.

As Brad hit his mid-thirties, he was asked by the elders of our church to be the leader of the mission team. He wholeheartedly accepted that role. Over the next five years, he spent time learning about each foreign field mission ministry that our church family supported with prayer and financial support. During that time, he became convinced that the real way to help our church family develop a "heart" for mission work was to take them to a field of service.

Determining Mexico would be the easiest place to go for cost and time, he began to take teams down to work with established national workers ministering along the northern Mexican Border with the United States. As first men, then women, and teens began to go on these trips, the enthusiasm for the work in Mexico began to move through our church family with excitement, and people who we would never expect to go on a trip to a foreign place to work would make the commitment and go and minister there.

I had just delivered our last child, our son, three weeks before his very first trip to Mexico. That meant that on early mission trips to Mexico, I was unable to go. When that son was four years old, I also began to go twice a year with Brad to work.

One day, after Brad had returned from a two-week trip to Mexico without me, he came into the kitchen and said, "I need to talk with you."

"Okay," I said. "Is it something serious? You sound serious." He asked me to sit down in the dining room chair. (You know that amped up my thinking, "This must be something very serious.")

He began, "I have hoped you have noticed this, but in case you haven't, I need to tell you now that for a long time I have felt great love for the Mexican people we have been ministering with in Mexico. I have been thinking about that and praying about that, and I have become convinced that we need to sell everything we have and move to the Mexican Border to minister alongside our brothers and sisters there in Christ. Before you say anything," he continued, "We have life here very comfortably. We have parts of both of our families right down the street or a few miles away. We have a good public school that the children are involved in. Our church family is faithful, loves God, is reaching the lost, and is nurturing all of us in our faith. I have been able to provide sufficiently for us here with my two jobs. But I think it's time we live at a higher level of faith. We are just too comfortable! I believe our family needs to learn and understand the very real need to trust God fully, instead of doing and providing for ourselves as we have. I think that can be achieved by selling all we have and moving to the border of Mexico and ministering there full-time."

I was speechless! I had been praying for years for spiritual growth that would be an internal transformation in our lives, more than in doing things in life. I had been waiting sometimes with hope, but oftentimes with frustration and doubt.

As I spoke, I remember finding it odd that I spoke with affirmation and praise for his conviction and complete agreement with his thoughts concerning moving our family to Mexico to minister there. We agreed to take a couple of weeks to pray together about this new conviction before speaking with our children.

A month or so later, we decided the time was right to speak to our children. At that time, our two oldest daughters were both away at Christian Colleges. We spoke to both, and they were delighted! "Go for it, Mom and Dad," they said. We then spoke to the other four younger children, aged 7 to 17. They had lots of questions. We answered the questions we had answers to, and Brad told them, "We will trust God for the other details." Everyone said they were on board and ready to start moving toward this great family adventure.

The next step was to approach our church elders for their blessing and accountability. They gave neither. That surprised us! It never dawned on us that those who loved us from our church family and with whom we had ministered might think we were "crazy." But they did, and stated as much!

We had multiple properties to sell. Brad had begun buying and restoring homes and would sell them under a real estate contract so they could provide retirement income. We had been doing that for about 5 years and had 2 properties to liquidate before our home. A property Brad had previously remodeled suffered rain damage during the 1991 Mississippi flood. We had handled the damage at the time of the storm, but now, two years later, the homeowners filed a lawsuit against Brad's remodeling business. It was for long-term, serious mold damage resulting from the flood waters. The amount of the lawsuit? The exact amount we estimated we would have as "cash out" to begin our life on the Mexican Border when all properties were sold.

We made a trip to the Mexican border to find a home that would meet both the needs of our family, but also serve as a mission lodging place for mission work teams coming and going back and forth between the U.S. and Mexico. We had a small, adequate place; we were planning to close on it when all things were sold and packed, and we were ready to move.

I called the day we packed the moving van to confirm our closing on the property, scheduled for two days away. The mortgage company had decided that since they could not verify income, which was from supporters and not documentable, they would need another 10% down for the property and would raise our interest rate 2%. Brad said, "We will not honor the contract, as those terms were not part of our agreement."

Each of the above incidents and so many more, less significant ones, came into our lives in the two years we prepped to go to the field. I often felt like it was "costing us" too much! *Why does God not clear the way for this to happen?* This was my naïve question. Brad seemed stable and diligent in moving forward, no matter what came our way. He simply trusted God to meet our needs. But this was a whole new way of looking at life for me. However, because of his faith and trust in God for all of these matters, I had peace as I realized my lifelong prayers for our family were coming true in real life. My husband had grown into a man of leadership with relentless trust and faith in God. I was learning to be patient, to wait on the Lord, and to live with complete trust in God and not from working with our own understanding.

I was amazed at the freedom and peace I felt as I followed my husband, Brad, with complete trust in God's work in our lives.

Those issues that presented themselves during our preparation to go to the field? God was working in each of them while we waited, prayed, and trusted Him for His movement.

- The Church elders? They asked to meet with us again. They apologized for being "afraid" of what we were doing and what that would require from them as a church family. They ended up blessing us, holding a commissioning service for the whole church and ourselves, and financially supporting that mission work in Mexico.

- The property we were being sued on, which showed the amount of the suit, was the same amount we had hoped to gain from complete liquidation. Our insurance settled with them out of court two days before our move.

- After we walked away from the contract on the house we planned to buy, we looked for another property. An old military chapel was converted into a church. We were able to buy that well-built 5,700-square-foot building for $12,000 in cash. With some remodeling and tweaking of the property, we ended up with a beautiful, adequate home and a large mission home to feed and lodge mission teams on the way in and out of Mexico. It met our needs way more than we ever could have imagined.

God was always working on the details....in our time of prayer and waiting.

It was a lesson that would present itself again and again in the 25 years we ministered in Mexico. We look back and feel the year of preparation for moving to Mexico was a "boot camp" of sorts, while we learned to really look to God for his direction, care, and provision, and then stepped into praying and waiting for his work.

One last season of waiting that I want to share with you. It was a very personal, heart-wrenching, and painful season. It was August of 2020, and Brad had been very ill. We were all living in the midst of the COVID pandemic. We originally thought that was what ailed him. Because of the way the medical world worked during those months, it was December before Brad was seen by a doctor and specialist. Within a few days, we had a pancreatic cancer diagnosis. It presented the best possible stage, 1a.

In the first part of 2021, he began a rigorous chemo treatment plan. In July, they had hoped that the Whipple surgery might give him considerably more time. One hour into the surgery, the surgeon called me to meet in the conference room. I knew when I saw his face. The blood arteries in the area that they would need to work on if they continued forward would cause him to bleed out. They were going to close him up. There was nothing more that could be done.

Our adult children had been sitting in our van in the hospital parking garage, moving in and out of the hospital every two hours to be with me, while I waited during the surgery and then during the following days for recovery. COVID restrictions would not initially let anyone else in but me, but the hospital made an exception as they considered this an "end of life" need, when they realized I had just had a heart attack two weeks prior and should have the children with me. He recovered well from that surgery and a month later, entered radiation. Radiation did irreparable damage to his digestive system. He fought long and hard to stay present with our family, but when God called him home on April 28, 2022, he expectantly and willingly left for His Father's Care. He had been reaching up towards Heaven for days.

Our family of seven adult children, one later adopted, their mates, our 28 grandchildren, and other friends and family gathered within three days to celebrate his life. As I sat there and memories were shared of his life, I could clearly see all the ways, all the times, God had worked in our lives during the waiting time.

It was the biggest heartbreak of my life, but it was the most glorious celebration of how and what God can provide for us here on earth, until we go on to meet our Creator in Eternity.

P.S. Though Brad and I were not spiritually equally yoked in the beginning of our marriage, God continued faithfully and diligently to pursue each of us individually to live with great trust in Him, not leaning on our own understanding.

The day we first met with the surgeon, we stopped at Cracker Barrel to eat on the way home. As we waited for our food, he grabbed my hand and said, "This is the day the Lord has made; the next days, weeks, months, are going to be difficult, but we will rejoice in each and every day." Ah, that husband of mine, giving me directives for how we would live through the most difficult season of our lives.

We went away to the mountains for a couple of days in February before his passing. He broke down there, crying, "Here we are. I am no longer capable of making love to you, providing for you, caring for you, being your husband. I am so grateful you honored me by being my wife."

A week before his last hospital visit, we were sitting on opposite sides of the sofa, talking casually. I slid over next to him. He put his arm around me and said, "For many years, you have leaned on my physical, emotional, and spiritual strength. I was honored by that; my strength was made perfect in my help with your weakness. I need you now to transfer your allegiance totally and completely to Jesus Christ only, for the strength you will need in the days ahead."

I had no idea, then, how much I would need his words in the days and years to come.

Next Steps:

As I break the verse down that was the source of this chapter, I find four things we can do to learn to trust God.

- Trust the Lord with all of your heart...This is both a movement of our mind and also a commitment of our will.

- Do not lean on your own understanding....for years, this was way more comfortable for me. I guess it was that "control" that we think we have. I learned that my own heart could be deceitful, my thoughts could be more self-serving. Only leaning into God's directive made it possible for me to trust Him.

- In all your ways acknowledge Him. I don't know why we have to be reminded to do this. But I sure did. I give him all the glory for the times of pain, hardship, waiting, and learning to trust him.

- He will make your ways straight. I could never have predicted the outcome of our life together. I thought we were a young farm couple raising a family in rural America. Instead, our life's work brought many people into a saving relationship with Jesus Christ. One of the great works God did through that time was hold our own children and family, steady in faithfulness, despite the struggles.

Say Yes to Trusting God!

- Don't wait. He is faithful, He is just, He loves us, and has provided for our greatest need with the gift of His Son. He can be trusted!

- Look for a way you can step out of your comfort zone and really give yourself an environment to trust God.

Grace for the Slow Healer: 3 Questions for Waiting Seasons

By Kristy Howard

"BE PATIENT TOWARD ALL THAT IS UNSOLVED IN YOUR HEART AND TO TRY TO LOVE THE QUESTIONS THEMSELVES."
RAINER MARIA RILKE

The West Texas sky spread overhead like an endless dome, wrapping our little homestead in a gentle embrace of light and just a hint of warmth. It was early April, and I was up to my wrists in the cool, moist dirt of our soon-to-be garden.

I wasn't alone. My husband, Jeremy, was nearby with the tiller, and our two little girls were at my elbows, "helping" me pull weeds from the soil on our five-acre homestead.

I watched as my six-year-old confidently tugged a green stem, breaking it off at ground level and tossing it onto a pile of weeds. Her three-year-old sister watched carefully, then followed suit, proudly holding up her own little prize.

"Let's do it how Daddy showed us," I suggested, lifting my spade out of the soil. "We have to get the roots out too, or the weeds just come back."

The girls watched as I thrust my spade back into the earth and extracted a tangled weed from the dark patches of clay and grit. Excitedly, they reached for their own little spades and started digging.

I watched my daughters for a minute, then glanced at our one-year-old son–seated like a tiny king on his throne of dirt. Both of his chubby hands were clasped around clods of soil. He grinned at me, and a chunk of dirt dribbled out of his mouth.

I grinned back and wiped his muddy face with his bib. This one was the family test-taster, especially of inedible things.

Eventually, the girls grew bored of the weeds and ran off to play.

My hands settled into the rhythm of prodding stubborn roots out of the unbroken soil, and my mind drifted toward the mental rut that had dominated my waking moments for too long.

Lord, I'm really blessed and really thankful. Thank You for my husband and our healthy kids. I'm not trying to be ungrateful, really. It's just...

My thoughts trailed off, the unfinished sentence hovering in the air around me. Tears stung my eyes.

It's just...why am I so unhappy?

When God Started Digging

It was a question my easygoing husband had asked more than once, and one that spiraled through my subconscious daily.

And I never had a good answer. Only more guilt.

I'm so frustrated, and I don't even know why.

The emotional darkness that always accompanied this thought crept over me. Despite the mild day, I felt myself shiver.

Tears dripped onto my dirt-stained knuckles, and I brushed at my eyes with annoyance. "I should be wearing the gloves Jeremy gave me," I muttered, suddenly in a huff.

But pulling weeds while wearing stiff leather gloves was nearly impossible. My fingers were much more nimble at reaching deep into the hard soil and digging out those stubborn little roots.

I dug at them now with the energy of pent-up frustration.

God, why? I try so hard...

This time, He didn't let me finish.

Kristy, you've been pulling at weeds in your life for years. I'm going to help you get rid of the roots.

I glanced up at the warm sky, almost expecting to find God looking directly down at me. Nothing but faint sun rays and my girls' happy voices met my senses in the gentle spring air.

But my heart—more than my ears—burned with those inaudible words:

I'm going to help you get rid of the roots.

He said it again, and this time I slumped over my bent knees in the soil. Tears warmed my dirt-caked hands as my little boy watched with those bright, curious eyes.

"Mama's okay," I said, dashing at my tears.

Andthen I laughed, and more tears sprang to replace them. "Mama's definitely going to be okay."

My little boy grinned and stuffed a clod of dirt into his mouth.

A Seed of Hope

At twenty-seven, I was willing to admit that I was *really frustrated*. And that was the understatement of the year. What I couldn't bring myself to say then, but would eventually be able to name, were words like chronic anger, anxiety, and depression.

Hardly a fitting description for a "good Christian" wife and mom. And I was a pastor's wife to boot, which meant I was supposed to be an *example*.

I hated how often I lost my temper and how miserable and guilty I felt all the time. If I wasn't losing my cool, then I was likely awake in the middle of the night, journaling or blogging about trying to do better. I always wanted to do better. To be better. I *expected* myself to be better, and that was the most frustrating thing of all.

I was stuck. And I hated myself for it.

So that April day—when God nearly split the big Texas sky and whispered a promise into the soil of my weary heart—it felt like my own personal revival, right there in that garden.

I was going to be a new person. I was finally going to be better, happier, more loving.

For the first time in a long time, the tears falling from my tired eyes were infused with hope, not hopelessness.

Thank you, God.

I whispered it while bathing my babies that night. And again, when I tucked them into bed. And again, when I kissed Jeremy goodnight and let my head sink into my pillow.

I closed my eyes and let hope embrace me. It felt good.

God is a really good Father. He's a healer of broken things. Things like good Christian girls with big, messy emotions and tired minds.

But God doesn't hand us the fine print. I think He knows we might never sign up for the cure if He did.

Instead, He invites us to trust Him. To take healing one messy step at a time.

Like a gardener thrusting a spade into the soil, over the next ten years, God's faithful hands gently, but thoroughly, tore apart the carefully constructed belief systems I had built my life upon.

And one by one, He removed roots from my heart.

Honestly, yanking weeds at ground level had felt easier. The garden of my life looked better that way, too. People liked my garden. It looked well-kept. People looked up to me. And as I said, I was a pastor's wife. I worked hard to live up to the good example expectation. But pretty gardens can still hide dry soil and overworked roots. I was surrounded by people and responsibility, but not by safe places to fall apart.

I served our little congregation faithfully, even as loneliness quietly pressed me to the breaking point. And oh, the energy it took to keep pulling weeds.

No wonder I was frustrated all the time. No wonder I felt relieved—so hopeful—when God promised to do something deeper.

But digging up roots was about to get messy. I don't know what I expected to happen when God whispered, *I'll help you get rid of the roots.*

Maybe I'd wake up with a new heart.
Moral perfection.
Instant peace.

What I didn't expect was a mental, physical, and emotional breakdown at twenty-nine. A two-year bout with depression that nearly took me under. Ongoing marriage stress, parenting stress, and financial stress. Church hurt that nearly broke us all.

I reminded God many times, during sobbing spells on the bathroom floor or long jogs where I tried to outrun the pain.

"You said You'd dig up the roots," I whispered. "Please... do it with gentler hands."

But healing doesn't always feel hopeful. And waiting rarely feels fruitful. And yet, hope—and growth—was exactly what God was unearthing in me.

Three Questions I Learned to Ask While Waiting

There are three important questions I've learned to live and ask (again and again) when I find myself in an uncomfortable waiting season.

Sitting with these questions helps me go from a place of feeling stuck, overwhelmed, and isolated–to embracing agency and purpose, even in the middle of hard seasons that feel anything but fruitful.

I'm not going to say that the waiting seasons of my life are over. Or that God has dug up *every* sinful root in my life. Because neither of those statements is remotely true.

But in the years that followed, I began learning to live the questions.

1. What if your healing doesn't look like hers?

This question started out as a fear: *What if I'm behind?*

You see, I spent years believing I was behind: I had a phobia of driving until I was in my early 30s. I had my first job interview in my mid-30s. I went back to college to finish my degree in my 40s.

Always behind. Behind in growth, behind in healing, behind in being the woman I thought I *should* be by now.

I watched other women move forward, grow, and step into roles I felt God calling me into. But I wasn't there yet. Not in healing. Not in peace. Not in purpose.

And I honestly felt like I'd never arrive. Have you ever felt this way, too?

The comparison game will keep you wrongly assuming that God has a different (better, faster) plan for everyone else.

That you're indefinitely stuck, or so far behind that you'll never experience meaningful growth in your personhood or your calling.

But healing isn't a race. And comparison is a thief: of joy, healing, creativity, and growth. Choosing to live fully into each messy day is really the key that unlocks the power of God's deepest healing and joy.

Solomon said it this way,

...I've had a good look at what God has given us to do—busywork, mostly. True, God made everything beautiful in itself and in its time—but he's left us in the dark, so we can never know what God is up to, whether he's coming or going. I've decided that there's nothing better to do than go ahead and have a good time and get the most we can out of life. That's it—eat, drink, and make the most of your job. It's God's gift.

Ecclesiastes 3:9-13, The Message

"God's gift" includes today - mine, and yours. *This moment. This mess.*

These days, I ask myself the question this way: "*So what* if your healing doesn't look like hers?" It's more of a permission slip than a question. Permission to thrive right here, right now. In this moment, this space, with confidence and purpose. To embrace all the broken days of healing as *God's gift*, even when today feels like dormant soil.

Easier said than done? I agree. The next question helps calm the inner hustle.

2. Am I trying to rush what God knows needs more time?

I like results, and quickly. When it comes to emotional growth and healing, it's easy to prefer a quick fix instead of living with the pain or disappointment.

Anxiety was a weed I'd tried to extract from my life *for years*. Long before I could name it, I was trying to work around it. In other words, pretend it wasn't there, so I didn't have to stop and dig it up.

But when the breakdown hit me at 29 (about a year after that day in the garden), I could no longer step around my issue. It was full stop time.

I ended up sitting in a little office, in a little town in Texas, and admitting in a little voice, "I'm not okay."

My counselor didn't diagnose me right away. But she did help me find the courage to begin unearthing those ugly roots beneath the symptoms I'd been frantically pulling at for nearly three decades.

Healing may not look like what you expected.

Instead of a three-step fix, growth may look like awkward talks with a counselor, hard conversations with your husband (and/or your kids), hours of journaling, long walks, heavy days, and facing what you fear the most–for me, that included everything from driving and making friends to talking on the phone and trying new things.

I was a mess, and the roots were deep and tangled. And the worst part? No one knew I was falling apart on the inside because, so far, everything still looked okay on the outside.

Honestly, I wanted to quickly get to the freshly-cut bouquets and fruit.

But God kept pulling me back into the garden shed to pull on my work gloves and get back to tending the soil of my life.

There was no rushing this. Only deep, sometimes painful healing, as old roots slowly lost their grip and new seeds of truth and grace took hold. There was *so much* unlearning and relearning, over and over again. Lies I had believed about my worth, my identity, my roles as a Christian woman. Misunderstandings I had about grace and guilt, and the provision of inner rest and confidence that was mine because of Jesus Christ.

There were many setbacks. Many *not-okay* days and nights.

For me, healing from anxiety and depression has looked like a lifetime of heart-tending through many seasons of planting, dormancy, growth, and fruitfulness. Hardly an overnight spectacular.

I used to think hope was a feeling. Now I know—it's a decision. A slow, messy, sometimes tear-soaked one.

Like the night I woke up in the middle of a panic attack...

3. Can I still hope, even when nothing feels better yet?

It wasn't the first time I'd experienced a night terror.

Although I wasn't familiar with the term yet, the feelings of *terror* were all too common: nightmares, panic, sweating, and heart racing.

I bolted upright out of bed, gasping for the next breath of air. The room was dark and still. I could sense more than hear the quiet breathing of my husband beside me and our youngest son in the crib across the room.

We were a few months into a move from that quiet little homestead in West Texas to a bustling suburb near the Dallas metroplex. Anxiety had followed me, like a faithful shadow that haunted by day and terrorized at night.

Months of sickness during my last pregnancy had morphed into chaotic post-partum hormones. Depression had slipped through the cracks, anxiety had split open in my psyche, and some days I wondered if I'd ever feel okay again. At night, I didn't even wonder.

As I stared into the darkness that night, something rose up inside of me, seemingly out of nowhere. Without even realizing what I was doing, I threw aside my quilt and nearly bolted from the bed.

I did something that night I hadn't been able to do in nearly two years—I faced the darkness. And yes, I mean the dark room. I was terrified of the dark at this point, as it seemed to magnify the inner darkness I had not been able to escape.

My heart racing, I walked into the hallway and stepped into the pitch black of our tiny living room. A righteous anger boiled up inside of me and burst out in an audible prayer. I leaned my head against the front door of our little rental home and wept uncontrollably.

That night, something changed in me. It was like I drew a line in the sand and *chose* to believe that I was being rebuilt, even when it felt like I was still falling apart.

Words from Psalm 31 began to wash over me:

Trapped by a siege, I panicked.
'Out of sight, out of mind,' I said.
But you heard me say it,
you heard and listened.

Love God, all you saints;
God takes care of all who stay close to him,
But he pays back in full
those arrogant enough to go it alone.

Be brave. Be strong. Don't give up.
Expect God to get here soon.

Psalm 31:22-24, The Message

Like David, author of Psalm 31, maybe you often panic or try to go it alone.

But that night, and many days since, I rose up and chose hope, rather than give in to despair and darkness. Is it time for you to take that stand, too?

"Expect God to get here soon."

That's the poignant answer to, *"Can I still hope, even when nothing feels better yet?"*

Yes. Yes, you can. And you must.

Grace for the Slow Healer

If you're in a season of waiting—for relief, clarity, healing, or peace—please hear this:

God is not absent in your waiting.
He is not punishing you.
He is not disappointed in you.
And He has not forgotten His promise.

He may be doing a deeper work than you expected. A slower work than you hoped.

God is a slow healer.

The roots may be deep, but so is His love. And God often digs deep to heal what we hide. So even if today feels like dormant ground, know that your Heavenly Father is tending something good in you.

As for me, I haven't reached the end of the healing story. Or the waiting season, honestly. I'm learning to stay in the soil—patient with the process, and tender toward the questions. Always believing that,

> "...God who started this great work in you would keep at it and bring it to a flourishing finish on the very day Christ Jesus appears."
>
> Philippians 1:6, The Message

Journal Prompt

- What buried pain or beliefs (roots) might God be gently uncovering in your heart right now?

- Where are you tempted to rush ahead rather than trust His slow, deep work?

- What would it look like to let hope be a deciding factor in your journey right now?

Prayer:

Father, I want to trust You with the parts of me that feel unfinished. When I grow weary in the waiting, remind me that You are patient and present. Help me stay open, stay honest, and stay near You. Give me grace for what's still healing, and hope for what's still coming.

In Jesus' name I pray, Amen.

Chapter 8

The Pit

By Kim "Sparrow" Spencer

HE LIFTED ME OUT OF THE PIT OF DESPAIR, OUT OF THE MUD
AND THE MIRE. HE SET MY FEET ON SOLID GROUND AND
STEADIED ME AS I WALKED ALONG.
PSALM 40:2, NLT

The door slams shut behind me. The past lies on the other side, locked tight—no going back. I stand at the edge of this giant, seemingly impassable crevasse. Looking down into nothing but darkness to a bottomless pit full of the unknown. Across what feels like miles and miles of "not yet".

The Bible tells us in the Old Testament that there was a young man named Joseph, who also once stood at the edge of a dark crevasse, a dark pit, wondering what was going to happen. Joseph was shoved over into that darkness by his own family -his older brothers. The brothers had such deep jealousy of him and a hatred in their hearts because of Joseph's relationship with their father, Jacob, who loved Joseph very much. Because of that deep hatred, they lured him to that pit and shoved him over, tore up his beloved coat of many colors, and told their Dad that a lion had killed their little brother.

Have you ever had anyone do you dirty like that—a trusted family member or friend? Well, Joseph's situation only got worse; he was then pulled out of the pit, sold into slavery, and taken to the land of Egypt.

There he served in the house of a high-ranking official. He did a wonderful job and did his work "as unto the Lord." "Work willingly at whatever you do, as though you were working for the Lord rather than people" (Colossians 3:23, NLT).

Ever feel frustrated in your work environment? What about that annoying co-worker or overbearing boss? Well, Joseph's story gives new meaning to the term 'toxic work environment'! Just like Joseph, we try to keep our heads up, look for the sunny side, and do the best we can in the difficulties we face in our "waiting".

Joseph was quite good-looking, and he caught the eye of the lady of the house. When she attempted to grab him, longing for an encounter, he ran out, leaving her holding his jacket! Of course, that rejection didn't sit well with her, and in the middle of him trying to do the right thing in a wrong situation, while he was waiting on the Lord, he ended up being sent to prison! Do you ever feel like that? You haven't done anything wrong, but all the doors just keep closing. You keep getting punished for something you didn't do, or at least it feels like your current situation is a punishment.

The Bible speaks highly of Joseph, but we know he was a human with feelings, just like us. When he found himself in a situation I'm sure he would've preferred not to be in, the Bible doesn't tell us for sure, but we know he had to feel disappointment, despair, frustration, and wanting to give up at times, maybe even saying, "Why me, Lord? Will You ever hear my cry for help?"

We're all humans, and our feelings come from the Lord. He created us with feelings. Jesus was fully human and fully God, walking the Earth, and He understands our feelings. So just like Joseph, we're going to be disappointed and frustrated and feel despair while we're waiting for God to open a path or intervene.

But rest assured, He does hear and He is making a way, dear child of God!

As the story continues, Joseph was gifted by the Lord to interpret dreams, and he interpreted the dream of the Pharaoh of Egypt, the most powerful person on earth at that time in history, in a way that no one else could. So that over a period of time, as he did his work "unto the Lord", while he waited, he came to hold the second-highest position in the land during a bad famine! Wow! That gives me hope for my situation!

From the pit to prison to the pharaoh's right-hand man!

Have you ever experienced something like this? You can't explain it, but you know you didn't open that window of opportunity, but without being in the "wrong" place at the right time, you couldn't have stepped into the next chapter of your story. This happened to me recently.

In North Carolina, where we live, a bad ice storm was heading our way. When I left work late that night, the dashboard of my 5-year-old Subaru lit up with what is often referred to as "the Christmas tree"—it's not a good Christmas tree—it means something is very wrong with the engine.

Once the dealership located the issue, the phone call went like this: Jack, the service department guy, said, "We located the problem."

"That's good," I replied.

"Not really," Jack said. From there, it went downhill very quickly!

The issue, according to Jack, was that I had not changed the oil as frequently as needed, which caused a very technical term, "gunk," to make the parts in the engine begin to fail. I would need a brand new engine in a 5-year-old car! Cost? At least $9,000 on a car, I still owed $15,000! And it was supposedly due to my not being as diligent as I should have been on oil changes. Listen, I am not out there weekly taking care of that automobile for sure - come on, it's there to serve my needs, but I know I did change the oil regularly and take care of the car in the same way I had previously taken care of all the cars I have driven over the past 40 years. Yes, I am at fault, but that's a steep price to pay!

While the ice storm kept rolling in, I got home and, while trying to remove the hose from the house, we broke the spigot, and water flooded our den. Fortunately, my sweet hubby had taught me where to find the water turn-off valve at the road, and we stopped the fire-hose level of water from pouring into the house. Three hours and $900 later, at 10 pm on a Saturday night, the plumber stopped the "bleeding." I woke up the next morning to an icy mess and a fresh case of pneumonia! All the while, my broken car still sits at the dealership.

What did I do to get into this mess? Some of my own doing and some not. I was in a money pit of bills, no transportation, and too sick to do anything about any of it. So I did the only thing I could: nothing. Instead, I left it with the Lord, and that is everything!

After speaking with the sales department at the dealership, they offered to purchase my poor, broken car and put me in a different, lovely, fully functioning vehicle—all for close to what I was already paying. How did this happen? I cannot explain it. I can say I had nothing to do with fixing it—I believe God opened the hearts and opportunities and minds of the people in charge and made a way.

It's just a car, and I felt silly and out of place asking Him to help me, but then my son said to me, "Mom, if Dad knew one of his children needed help, he would intervene. God is a good Father like that."

As I drove away in this miracle, I felt surrounded by God's provision for my daily needs. I felt His arms hugging me. I felt cared for and seen. The constant problems of this human condition are ever-changing, but our Father is never changing; He is always the same.

Well, my friend, God is writing that story for you, too! He is using all the things of this life; the good, the bad, and the ugly to draw us closer to His love while showing Himself to us in our circumstances, which oftentimes can only be done in "the pit". When things are working perfectly, there is not always the opportunity for God to show up BIG! When we get to the point where we can no longer "fix" ourselves, we are forced to turn to the only real help or hope in this world- the Lord. At this moment, we can start to see His plan unfold, and we feel like He has seen us and reached out to hold us. We feel His love.

We find out in Joseph's next chapter that the famine was so bad that his brothers traveled to Egypt—the same brothers who had shoved him into that dark pit 17 years earlier. These same brothers unknowingly begged the head of Egypt's food distribution department, AKA their little brother Joseph, for help to give them supplies and food, so they and all their nation would not perish.

Joseph saw that his brothers had come before him for an audience to beg for assistance. First, he put them through a few questions and tests (he was a human after all—maybe having a little "fun"), but he finally revealed himself to them. Having believed Joseph must have died years earlier, their minds were racing, wondering what he might do to them, the revenge they deserved, and he was now positioned to dish out. Joseph's waiting period had come to this epic moment-what would he do?

But Joseph shocked his brothers and said, "You intended to harm me, but God intended it for good to accomplish what is now being done, the saving of many lives" (Genesis 50:20). Joseph then embraced them, wept, and took care of them. Because even though the truth is his brothers had caused him great harm and deep pain, putting him in a terrible situation, where he waited for over 17 years, he knew that the Lord was the one in control, and most importantly, he knew that his hope was in the Lord! When we find ourselves waiting, and it seems like things are never going to change, the one place we can find Hope is in the promises of the Lord.

God is greater than our feelings. It's okay to have our feelings, but we need to remind ourselves and testify to ourselves that God is greater than our feeling- God is good, He loves us and He tells us, "For I know the plans I have for you," declares the Lord, "plans to prosper you, and not to harm you, plans to give you hope and a future" (Jeremiah 29:11).

Our loving Father has a plan: "...in all things God works for the good of those who love him, who have been called according to his purpose" (Romans 8:28). This does not say that all things are good. When Joseph went through his dark moments, he had to be hurting emotionally and physically. We hurt through our dark times, too. The pain of this life is very real. But God has a plan to use even those difficult times. We can stake everything on His promises, and we can, like Joseph, say that "what the enemy meant for evil, God will use for good."

If God is for you, who can be against you? Look for God "winks" in your waiting period: the slightly open window of opportunity, the warm hug of a stranger, the unexpected money in the mail—all these and so much more are the breadcrumbs of our good Father feeding His sparrows—feeding you, His beloved!

Chapter 9

Hope In The Waiting: Finding Purpose and Joy In The Waiting

By Julie Davis

ANSWER ME SPEEDILY, O LORD; MY SPIRIT FAILS! DO NOT HIDE YOUR FACE FROM ME, LEST I BE LIKE THOSE WHO GO DOWN INTO THE PIT. CAUSE ME TO HEAR YOUR LOVINGKINDNESS IN THE MORNING, FOR IN YOU DO I TRUST; CAUSE ME TO KNOW THE WAY IN WHICH I SHOULD WALK, FOR I LIFT UP MY SOUL TO YOU. DELIVER ME, O LORD, FROM MY ENEMIES; IN YOU I TAKE SHELTER. TEACH ME TO DO YOUR WILL, FOR YOU *ARE* MY GOD; YOUR SPIRIT *IS* GOOD. LEAD ME IN THE LAND OF UPRIGHTNESS. PSALM 143:7-10, NKJV

I never expected my life to unfold in the waiting. As a young girl who came to Christ early, my faith was bright, simple, and full of certainty. I believed with all my heart that loving the Lord meant the road ahead would be smooth and clearly marked. In my youthful understanding, obedience would surely lead to predictable blessings and a happily-ever-after life.

I held tightly to this promise:

"For I know the thoughts that I think toward you, says the Lord, thoughts of peace and not of evil, to give you a future and a hope."

Jeremiah 29:11, NKJV

I clung to it with bright confidence, certain the future would unfold exactly as I hoped.

While many of my friends were dreaming of ambitious careers, my dream was beautifully simple: get married, have a family, serve in ministry like my parents, and live a life fully devoted to God. When I met the man I would marry during college, it felt as though everything was unfolding exactly according to plan.

But growing up has a way of gently—and sometimes painfully—reshaping what we thought we understood.

It did not take long to discover that life is far more complex than my younger self imagined. Prayers were not always answered on my timetable. Doors I expected to swing open remained firmly shut. Seasons of waiting stretched longer than my faith felt comfortable holding.

And slowly, humbly, I learned a trust that would shape the rest of my journey: Life is simply too complex to live well without Christ.

Even in those early seasons of uncertainty, God was quietly at work. Through the noise and confusion, His presence brought a calm in the waiting I could not explain. He provided strength when I felt weak, wisdom when I felt unsure, and a growing love for Him and for serving others. Looking back, I can now see that God was already meeting me in the waiting, turning my uncertainty into hope long before I recognized what He was doing.

During this time of waiting, these verses began to speak deeply into my heart:

> "Then you will call upon Me and go and pray to Me, and I will listen to you. And you will seek Me and find *Me*, when you search for Me with all your heart. I will be found by you," says the Lord, "and I will bring you back from captivity; I will gather you from all the nations and from all the places where I have driven you," says the Lord, "and I will bring you to the place from which I cause you to be carried away captive."
>
> Jeremiah 29:12-14, NKJV

Over the years, my husband and I were blessed to serve in several church ministry positions. We were a team, united in purpose and calling. Time and again, God had restored our joy in seasons of waiting, and we learned to trust His faithfulness.

So when we were offered a ministry opportunity in a new community, we stepped forward with anticipation and hope. But this time, something felt different. At first, it was only a quiet uneasiness, the kind you try to dismiss. I noticed I was no longer included in the ways I had been before. When I gently expressed concern, I was reassured that everything was fine. Still, the heaviness in my spirit would not lift.

Before long, others began noticing what I had sensed.

What followed was one of the most painful seasons of my life. Evidence came to light. The church asked my husband to resign. He blamed me for what had happened. Despite my desire to pursue counseling and restoration, he chose to end our marriage.

Within a year, I found myself divorced.

Suddenly, I was standing in a life I had never imagined. My marriage was gone. My four wonderful children were grown and building their own lives. The dreams I had carried for decades lay in pieces at my feet. I was not only grieving what I had lost, but I was also grieving what I believed would never be.

Questions I never thought I would ask began to rise quietly in my heart. Where are You, God?

What am I supposed to do now?

My faith felt fragile, my prayers felt like whispers into silence. Joy seemed like a distant memory. What was I to do with my life? How was I going to go into this chapter of life? I had never known life as a single person. I wrestled with confusion and sorrow, and wondered if God truly saw me in the depths of my heartbreak.

In the middle of my pain, God revealed His deep compassion, steadfast love, and gentle presence, meeting me not with condemnation for my questions, but with grace for my wounded heart. This is where I was going to see and experience the love of God in the deepest, most intimate way. I was going to begin learning what it means to lean on Him when you don't have answers, and you don't know what is coming.

God met me in my waiting. He gently taught me to be still.

"Be still, and know that I *am* God; I will be exalted among the nations, I will be exalted in the earth."

Psalms 46:10, NKJV

Waiting was no longer empty space to endure; it became sacred ground where God met me personally.

Day by day, my hope began to breathe again. Not because the pain instantly disappeared, but because God faithfully redeemed it. He taught me to trust again, to walk by faith when answers were still unseen, and to face each new morning with quiet confidence that I was held securely in His hands.

"Fear not, for I *am* with you; be not dismayed, for I *am* your God. I will strengthen you, yes, I will help you, I will uphold you with My righteous right hand."

Isaiah 41:10, NKJV

His presence in my waiting turned my uncertainty into a new hope for the future.

Joy– real, steady joy– began to return to my weary heart.

Now may the God of hope fill you with all joy and peace in believing, that you may abound in hope by the power of the Holy Spirit.

Romans 15:13, NKJV

God restored my life in ways I could never have orchestrated. I found meaningful places to serve again. I had precious time with my parents, my children, and my grandchildren. My life was full in many beautiful ways, yet I still felt the quiet ache of loneliness.

And then, in His perfect timing, God did what only He can do. Just as I was learning contentment in singleness, He brought into my life a wonderful man who, like me, had been faithfully walking with God through his own season of waiting after divorce. It did not take long to recognize what God had been preparing in both of us. God has blessed us through the blending of our families and provided for us in ways I never imagined. For me, this has been one of the deepest times of growth in my life. The same God who met me in my waiting, who restored my hope, who healed my heart, had been writing a new chapter all along. Today, I can say with deep conviction: waiting was never wasted. God used every tear, every question, every uncertain step to grow me, refine me, and draw me closer to His heart. He restored my joy. He rebuilt my hope. He strengthened my faith in ways comfort never could.

Take heart, God meets us in the seasons of waiting. His presence turns uncertainty into hope. And in His perfect time, He restores joy to our weary hearts.

Waiting on the Lord during a season of devastation through the divorce of my first husband has been both painful and sacred. Walking through divorce stripped away what once felt stable and secure. It forced me into a place of deep surrender. In the quiet, I began to understand waiting was not passive–it was an invitation to draw nearer to Jesus Christ and allow Him to redefine my life.

As everything familiar fell away, God gently revealed what life would look like with just Him and me. I learned that true independence was not found in self-sufficiency, but in complete dependence on Christ. The Holy Spirit became my teacher, guiding me day by day, shaping my heart, and growing me into greater Christlikeness.

Through this waiting, God has been building godly character within me—patience, humility, perseverance, and trust. What once felt like devastation has become a place of transformation. In this stillness, God showed me what it meant to walk independently—not apart from others in bitterness or isolation, but independently anchored in Him alone. I am learning to release expectations, approval, and reliance on anything other than Jesus Christ. The Holy Spirit is patiently teaching me, revealing areas that need healing, pruning, and growth.

As I waited, God was building something new within me. He shaped my character, refined my heart, and gave me clarity and direction I never knew before. This waiting season taught me to trust Him fully, to grow in Christlikeness, and to embrace a new purpose that is rooted not in my past, but in a deeper desire to reflect Christ in every area of my life.

The Lord had given me a new focus, renewed purpose, and a deeper desire to live fully for His glory. Even in the waiting, He had been faithful.

There are seasons in life when the questions outnumber the answers, when the heart aches for clarity and relief, yet the silence stretches on. It is in these moments—the waiting, the uncertainty, the unanswered prayers—that our faith is tested and refined. Walking by faith does not mean ignoring the pain or pretending we understand God's time; it means trusting Him even when we cannot see the path ahead. God meets us in the waiting. His presence can turn our uncertainty to hope while He gently restores joy in weary hearts. As we learn to trust Him without seeing the full picture, we discover that the waiting itself can become a sacred space where faith grows stronger and hope takes root.

God Meets Us In The Waiting

"The Lord is good to those who wait for Him, to the soul who seeks Him."

Lamentations 3:25,NKJV

Waiting can test our faith, patience, and trust in God.

Waiting on the Lord is never easy–especially when the waiting is born out of devastation. Seasons like divorce can leave us feeling disoriented, stripped of security, and uncertain about the future. Yet Scripture reminds us that waiting is not wasted time in God's economy. Often, it is in the deepest places of loss that the Lord does His most profound work.

This season of waiting forces us to confront what faith looks like when familiar support systems are gone. It reveals what life looks like when obedience replaces comfort, and when dependence on others is replaced by wholehearted reliance on Jesus Christ. I had grown up going to church, reading my Bible, and praying, yet I didn't want to do any of that anymore. The one man I had vowed to love until death had betrayed me, and I felt I could never trust again. Despite my feeling of not wanting to do any of this anymore, I did not allow myself to withdraw from going to church, reading my Bible, and praying. I was reminded that my first husband, just like everyone, is human and can disappoint us. But God never changes and is one I could depend on to be consistent. In the quiet, the Holy Spirit becomes our teacher–shaping our character, clarifying our purpose, and drawing us into a deeper walk with Christ. It is in our daily quiet time with Christ where He wants to speak to us. Often, Christ is seen as a "genie in a bottle," and our quiet time is spent with our wish list of things we want Him to do or provide. We spend all our time talking and very little time being still to listen for God to speak to our hearts.

I realized the importance of actually hiding God's word in my heart, so I would have ready access to His promises and provision in my mind and thoughts. It was through reading scriptures that I learned how much God loved me, how much He cared for me, and how He loves me so much He wants the very best for me and wants to bless me abundantly.

Waiting on God is not passive resignation; it is active trust. It is where God refines us, redirects us, and prepares us for what He is calling us into next. The biblical truth is that God uses waiting to shape our character, deepen our faith, and prepare us for His promises.

His Presence Turns Our Uncertainty Into Hope

We are all confronted with times of waiting. Whether in a line at the store, waiting for an appointment, or in traffic, we all have moments of waiting. And for many of us, the brief moments of waiting can be handled. Yes, there are times when we are inconvenienced by the waiting, but we see it as a slight inconvenience, something that will be over shortly.

However, there are times when waiting is more than a moment; it is for a season. And just as seasons in life are not defined with a particular time limit, so there are seasons of waiting.

In the long and often uncomfortable season of waiting, God is never absent; He is present, purposeful, and quietly at work, turning uncertainty into hope. David experienced this as he was anointed king while still a shepherd, only to spend years hiding in caves, fleeing from Saul, and waiting for God's promise to unfold–learning in the waiting that God's timing is as intentional as His calling.

Likewise, Joseph's life reveals how God's presence remains steady even when the path makes no sense. Sold into slavery by his own brothers, Joseph moved through stages of waiting that included servitude in Potiphar's house, betrayal and false accusation, imprisonment, and long years of forgotten promises. Though Joseph knew God had given him dreams of being used for something greater, the road toward them was marked by adversity and uncertainty that surely did not resemble deliverance or purpose in the moment. Yet at every stage–whether as a servant, a prisoner, or eventually a leader–God was shaping Joseph's character, positioning him for influence and preparing him to preserve life during a famine. What Joseph could not see then, God was faithfully orchestrating all along, transforming confusion into clarity and despair into hope. In our own waiting, as with David and Joseph, God reminds us that delay is not denial, and uncertainty is often the very place where hope is formed and trust in Him is deepened.

God has given us His Word, the Bible, to demonstrate His faithfulness in so many different situations. When we are lonely, God is there. When we feel lost and in despair, God is there to comfort and give us a peace that surpasses all understanding. It was that kind of comfort I began to experience while waiting. There was so much uncertainty about my future, yet God was there every step of the way. I soon discovered that in the midst of my deepest hurt, God was there every day and in so many ways. As I look back over my life, I have seen God's faithfulness, walking with me through the storm. All past evidence had proven Him faithful, and now I had to choose to believe and know God's faithfulness would be with me even now. Even when I didn't feel like praying, I prayed. When I didn't feel like reading my Bible, I still did. For when I was in God's word, learning His ways, seeing examples of His provision, His faithfulness, and His love, I had such comfort in knowing God was not going to leave me now. He was there to walk every step with me. He was there and helped me walk through the days when I didn't think I could walk one more step. He was my constant companion. I had to constantly choose to walk by faith, not by sight, and trust God to take care of the rest.

As the days turned into weeks, months, and years, I gained a renewed sense of hope and joy in my life. My happiness was not dependent on others or my circumstances; it came from my relationship with Jesus Christ. Through His word, He spoke to me. He was building in me a Christlike character to love life again. Not knowing all the details of my future was going to be okay because I knew God already knew my future and would prepare me for whatever I needed. There were still many details I didn't know, but I could face each new day boldly. God was my Hope in my time of waiting.

He Restores Joy To Our Weary Heart

Waiting seasons can feel heavy because they often strip away certainty, control, and clear direction. Yet Scripture shows us that God does not wait to restore our joy until our circumstances change—He restores it while we are still in the middle of the unknown. Biblical joy is not rooted in having answers about the future, but in trusting the One who already holds it. David prayed, "Restore to me the joy of Your salvation, and uphold me *by Your* generous Spirit." (Psalm 51:12, NJKV), not because His life was easy, but because He understood that joy flows from a relationship with God, not from resolved outcomes. When we wait, God gently shifts our focus from what we are waiting for to who we are waiting with. In that sacred space, joy begins to grow— not as excitement, but as a quiet confidence that God is present, faithful, and working even when we cannot see it.

So how do we find joy when the future feels uncertain? Joy is found by anchoring our hearts in God's character rather than our circumstances. We find joy when we choose to remain connected to Him through prayer, Scripture, worship, and gratitude, even when our questions remain unanswered. Joy often begins as a decision before it becomes a feeling—a choice to trust God's goodness, to believe His promises are still true, and to rest in the truth that He wastes nothing. James reminds us, "My brethren, count it all joy when you fall into various trials,"(James 1:2 NKJV), not because trials are pleasant, but because God is using them to mature and strengthen our faith.

And how will we know when we have found joy? Joy reveals itself not through the absence of fear or sadness, but through stability in the midst of them. You will know you have found joy when peace starts to coexist with uncertainty, when hope remains even without answers, and when your heart feels steady instead of frantic. Joy shows up as a deep assurance that God is enough–even if the waiting continues. It is the quiet strength that helps you get up each day, the ability to praise God before the promise is fulfilled, and the trust that whatever comes next, God will be faithful. This kind of joy is not loud or fleeting; it is rooted, resilient, and sustained by the presence of God Himself.

> In this you greatly rejoice, though now for a little while, if need be, you have been grieved by various trials, that the genuineness of your faith, *being* much more precious than gold that perishes, though it is tested by fire, may be found to praise, honor, and glory at the revelation of Jesus Christ, whom having not seen you love. Though now you do not see *Him*, yet believing, you rejoice with joy inexpressible and full of glory.
>
> 1 Peter 1:6-8,NKJV

Waiting on the Lord is one of the most challenging disciplines of the Christian life, especially when the waiting is not chosen but forced upon us by circumstances beyond our control. Seasons of devastation–such as divorce, betrayal, grief, or unexpected loss–have a way of dismantling what once felt safe, predictable, and secure. In these moments, waiting can feel less like spiritual formation and more like survival.

It's amazing how we think we know how our lives are supposed to go. Divorce, in particular, brings a unique kind of devastation. It not only ends a relationship but often shatters identity, dreams, expectations, and long-held assumptions about the future. What once defined life—family structure, shared callings, mutual support—suddenly dissolves. In its place stands uncertainty, vulnerability, and a deep ache for clarity.

But even all that could not be enough to separate us from the love of God. It is amazingly wonderful to see how God, in His infinite wisdom, knew we would create our own future and dreams for ourselves, but God had a plan for each of us. As a child of God, He protects us in ways we can't understand. He provides for us in ways we would never have imagined, and He walks with us each step of the way, guiding us, encouraging us, comforting us, and building in us Christ-like character along the way.

Waiting is often where God does His deepest work. It is where He meets us when distractions fall away, when voices grow quiet, and when we are left with a choice—cling to what was, or surrender fully to what God is doing now.

God provides us with a "road map" throughout the Bible. The Bible is filled with men and women who encountered God most powerfully in the season of waiting. Abraham waited for a promised son. Joseph waited through betrayal and imprisonment. David was anointed to be king, yet ran for his life, hiding in caves, before God allowed him to be King. Hannah waited in barrenness. Israel waited in exile. Even Jesus spent thirty years before beginning His public ministry. And in it all God gave them direction, peace, and joy in the waiting times of their lives. Through their examples, we can capture the same form of discernment, peace, and joy. In their seasons of waiting, as in our waiting, God was working. God was building character in them to prepare them for the next season of their lives. God provided them joy in the waiting. Not the kind of joy we know, but the kind of joy that only God can give. The joy and peace in the midst of waiting when we don't have the answers, we don't understand the circumstances and reasons, yet we know our Heavenly Father loves us so much He will never leave us alone in the waiting. And through each of those seasons of waiting, we come out closer to God, stronger in our faith, and more determined to live life according to God's plans for us and not our plans alone. His plans for us provide a far better life than we could ever give ourselves. When we learn to trust God in the uncertainty of life, in the chaos, disappointment, and despair in the waiting, we see God demonstrate His love for us as we could never have imagined.

NEXT STEPS

Waiting may feel like standing still, but in God's hands, it is a season of movement—heart work, soul work, and faith work. As you lean into Him, you will discover that the waiting itself is part of His loving plan to prepare you for what only He can bring.

> Trust in the Lord with all your heart, and lean not on your own understanding; In all your ways acknowledge Him, and He shall direct your paths.
>
> Proverbs 3:5-6, NKJV

Here is a short list of actionable encouragement:

- Anchor in God's Word - Speak His promises daily.

- Stay in Community –Let others hold you up in prayer.

- Guard Your Perspective–Remember God's past faithfulness

- Release Control–Surrender your timeline to His.

- Celebrate Small Steps–Recognize signs of His presence and progress

God Meets Us Personally in the Waiting

Waiting creates space for intimacy with God. In the quiet, His presence becomes clearer, His Word becomes more alive, and our relationship with Him deepens.

Self-Reflection:

- How has my prayer life or time in God's Word changed during this season?

- In what ways have I experienced God's nearness when everything else felt uncertain?

- Challenge Activity:

Commit to a daily quiet moment this week—even if brief—where you listen more than you speak. Write down anything God impresses on your heart through Scripture, prayer, or stillness.

His Presence Turns Our Uncertainty Into Hope

Waiting seasons are not pauses in our spiritual life; they are places where God does some of His deepest work. When life feels suspended, God is actively shaping our character, strengthening our faith, and preparing us for what lies ahead.

Self-Reflection:

- Where in my life do I feel "stuck" or delayed right now?

- How might God be using this waiting season to grow me rather than punish me?

- Challenge Activity:

Write a short prayer surrendering your waiting season to God. Ask Him to show you what He is forming in you, not just what He is withholding from you.

Self-Reflection:

- What character traits has God been developing in me during this waiting season?

- How have I grown spiritually compared to who I was before this season began?

Waiting Is Where God Restores Hope and Joy

Joy is not postponed until waiting ends—it is cultivated within it. God restores joy by reminding us that our hope is rooted in Him, not in circumstances.

Self-Reflection:

- What has brought me joy in this season that I might have overlooked?

- How has my understanding of joy changed through waiting?

- Challenge Activity:

Create a "Hope Journal" for this season. Each day or week, write one way you have seen God's faithfulness, presence, or provision. Revisit these entries when discouragement arises.

Waiting on a Dream:
Your Story is Your Voice

By Amber Rose

BE STILL BEFORE THE LORD AND WAIT PATIENTLY FOR HIM;
DO NOT FRET WHEN PEOPLE SUCCEED IN THEIR WAYS,
WHEN THEY CARRY OUT THEIR WICKED SCHEMES.
PSALM 37:7, NKJV

Til Death Do Us Part

As a writer, creating a fictional character from scratch is one of the most exciting elements of a good book. You ask yourself, what is their hair color, eye color, or height? What are their favorite foods, favorite hobbies, or favorite time of day? Who is their best friend? Who is their enemy? What sets your character on fire? What is their greatest weakness? What are their strengths? Then you ask yourself, as a writer, what is the worst thing that can happen to my character? Because when all seems lost, the core belief of that character starts to emerge, and they fight for what really matters to them. And that is the climax of your story.

From a young age, I could get lost in the world of my characters for hours. I'd get lost in my favorite author's books, too. Reality, however, is much, much different. And growing up in the real world is not nearly as defined as you see in books.

***

"What are all these old papers anyway?" "Do you really need all this stuff?" "I should keep some of these college textbooks. They may be outdated, but they are still useful," he went on. My husband and I stood in the upstairs bedroom of our 1,085-square-foot house. A national pandemic hit our country a few months ago. Pre-pandemic life was too busy to do all the things around the house and yard that were on his wish list, but now we could. We fought for over a year to get this little converted hunting cabin in a short sale so we could move out of a one-bedroom apartment and start a family. While everyone went into lockdown, this man set out to do as many house projects as possible. Since I was more 'handy' than he was, a lot of the house renovations fell on me, especially as I went on full-time unemployment for a bit between jobs. After weeks of outdoor and indoor house projects, he decided it was time to go through old boxes in the upstairs rooms. He wanted to have more kids, and this effort would make room for that.

The single upstairs window hung open, letting in the spring air, while the furnace lay silent behind a curtain in the largest room. I scanned the boxes of his old textbooks in the corner of the upstairs room, from where we stood around an 8-foot sorting table. "If we haven't touched something in three years, we probably don't need it," he quoted a friend. I said nothing. I learned early in our marriage not to question my husband's logic. His textbooks sat right where they had been for over two years. I looked at my own boxes of books and papers. This wasn't the first time I had to do a full purge. When I was in my teens, my family had to downsize to a new house, and we kids were told to get rid of as much as possible in case our living arrangements were too small for a family of seven. So, this exercise wasn't new to me; it was just a bit painful every time, as items tend to have memories attached to them.

Feeling good about his progress, he took a break from sorting and went downstairs to watch TV. He had made a donation pile, set items aside to sell online, and made a few piles of trash. I kept sorting through my own bins filled with old photographs, making a pile of children's books, stuffed animals, or toys for donation, sorting through grade school papers, and so many other stacks of paper. The nostalgia I felt as I sifted through each box of memories was overwhelming. Then something caught my eye. In between the stacks of old church bulletins, notes, and school archives, there was a manuscript. Stacks of papers, research, written and typed versions of an unfinished manuscript that piled up several inches high.

I found receipts from a road trip I took with a friend, researching areas I wanted to write about. There were early versions of my manuscript that I'd written but later changed. These stacks of typed and handwritten pages were what represented hours spent clicking away on my dad's old computer as a teen, or days spent creating fictional characters and stories. He didn't know I loved writing creatively. From a young age, I dreamed of becoming a published author. Early on in our marriage, I learned a few things about the man I married.

- He was more of a cat person than a dog person.

- Being self-employed (as I was early on in our marriage) or working a 1099 job wasn't something he would allow.

Therefore, my hidden dream of becoming a published author one day needed to remain just that...a dream. I never trusted this man enough to share my deepest secrets with him. Maybe it was the number of times he strangled me in a fit of rage. Or the way he made me feel as though everything that went wrong was my fault, or my job to find the resolution. Maybe it was because he was more educated than I, having attended an *Ivy League school* (as he put it). Or maybe something in my gut knew he couldn't be trusted? To the world, he was the most involved, family- and community-centered individual. Behind closed doors, he could turn into a fit of violent rage, smashing objects, walls, or slamming his fists onto his head in a maddened state of mind.

> *I didn't know that "till death do us part" meant death at his own hands...*
> *And death to freedom...*
> *And death to dreams...*

From my early teens, writing creatively was something that kept me awake at night. Story ideas would flood my mind midday. Despite the chaos that was my marriage and the physical, emotional, and mental abuse my child and I were living through, there was that underlying desire to write. Yet from a young age, I was groomed to become a good wife and mother. Being a good wife and mother meant putting your husband's and family's needs first, even before your own. Dying to self, you could say.

As I stood in that upstairs room, something in me snapped. I started to bundle all the papers up into a bag and tied it shut in a simple bowknot. Leaving everything else behind in various piles. I carried the bundle of papers downstairs and outside. As I passed him on the couch, he casually asked, "What's all that?" "Just junk," I quipped back and pushed through the front door. I walked around to the trash bins, opened the lid, and "plop," the years of manuscripts and research dropped to the bottom. Gone.

If hearts could crack, I think mine did. But I didn't let myself feel it. I'd learned to suppress my feelings when things in our marriage hurt too deeply. I went back inside and finished organizing things.

A piece of my writing may have died that day, but something new was forming beneath the surface. I just didn't know it yet.

From the Ashes, New Life Begins.

My marriage ended long before I realized my child and I needed to flee for our lives... Like a forest fire, violence had burned it to the ground.

You know the most amazing thing about forests after a fire, or the earth after a volcanic eruption? Life continues through the ash. New trees, plants, and flowers push up through the ash. Nature doesn't end when the fire has consumed everything in its path. Rather, it gives way for new life to form. But it's never the same.

There is hope after the fires end. I'm here to tell you, there is hope even when all seems lost.

In my last chapter with hope*books, *The Art of Letting Go*, I shared about moving forward from survival mode. I couldn't have written that piece without the help and support of some special individuals who inspired me to start writing again. During my abusive marriage, I had almost lost hope of becoming a writer. Once I got out of that unsafe environment and started to heal and move forward, a glimmer of hope reignited within me. Have you ever been in that place where those deepest dreams seem to be the farthest away, almost unattainable?

Moving forward from survival mode felt like a snake crawling out of old skin, or a potted plant, being sifted to move into new soil. Uncomfortable, restless, and unsettling. Looking back, I see where God was using my circumstances to remove old layers, or old versions of myself, to prepare me for the new experiences ahead. Sometimes, you must lose the old before you can receive the new. You can't pick up more grocery bags when your hands are full, because if you do, something is going to break, rip, or fall from your hands. I know you've tried it! Sometimes the waiting time is to give us a chance to shed the old layers before the new growth can emerge.

Waiting seasons are so important. Whether you're walking forward into a psychological battle in court, working through cancer in a hospital, tending to the daily tasks at home, raising your kids, working a job, or juggling school, sports, and more. You may find yourself in a season of waiting. If there isn't an answer and the solution isn't visible right away, stay focused on your goals. Let the season of waiting do its work. Keep pushing forward through the pressure. Because from the ashes come the purest and most beautiful things in nature, and our lives.

Your story is being written.

When a woman is in an abusive situation, her voice is often suppressed. It may have looked like I had an opinion to outside viewers, but on the inside, my voice was shut down and locked away. Not just my physical voice, but my written voice, too. My ex even dictated when and what was posted online. Only what my abuser wanted and wished for mattered. It was safer to follow his lead that way.

A few months after fleeing my abuser, I held in my hand a journal he had given me one holiday. "Write nice things about me in it," he told me when I opened the gift that day. It was the first journal where I started recording the abuse I had experienced in my marriage, and as I worked through my post-separation recovery. As I wrote the truth of my experiences, my writing grew; I stopped the recordings in my head by writing down the words and incidents, and I started to find my voice.

Healing can be very messy. It can also seem lonely when you are dealing with post-separation abuse, living day to day in survival mode. It was several years later, as I worked through the hard process of healing, that I started to feel like I was growing again. Every time I stood up for myself, my body would break down, get sick, or at times, I'd physically lose my voice. Often, in my healing journey, it felt like I was moving one step forward, two steps to the right, four steps back, one step forward, three steps to the left, five steps backward, two steps forward, one step back, one step forward....you get the idea.

They say that one in four women is a victim of domestic violence. When I hear things like that, I recognize the oppression that physically abusive relationships have on the soul. The control the abuser has over you, the manipulation of believing you're always in the wrong, and the mental gymnastics a woman does daily to anticipate the next explosion are unimaginable to most people living a normal life. To think about a dream while living in survival mode is impossible.

I've heard many women say they chose to stay. I see you. I hear you. But for me, staying meant death. Not just for me, but for my child. Leaving, for us, meant the ability to find peace, even if just a little bit. I wasn't worried about someone punching me in my sleep because I was snoring, or controlling how much we ate, how I wore my hair, what clothes I wore, how I spent my money, what photos or text I posted on social media for him, or where we did or didn't volunteer our free time, to name a few. For us, leaving meant staying alive.

If you are in an unsafe situation, please create a safety plan and make sure you have what you need to get out and get support from people around you before it's too late! If you think God values marriage over yours and your children's safety, you've been misled. God doesn't want you (or your kids) in an unsafe or life-threatening situation, so please get out if you are in danger!

For me, writing what I had experienced allowed me to pull the patterns and the events into the light. Whether someone would read my writing someday wasn't the point at the time. The point was to release those stories from my mind and free my brain from replaying those events over and over again. My abuser was notorious for twisting things so much that I believed I was always at fault or caused his explosions. Writing down the true stories gave me clarity, courage, and belief in myself that what I experienced was real. And coming through all of that took time, but it was worth the wait.

For my readers who have experienced physically violent and abusive relationships, you are stronger than you think. If you're like me, you may have had hopes and dreams that your abuser suppressed. There may be parts of you that you feel you have lost. But they are not lost. That new version of you is waiting with open arms.

Waiting looks different for each of us. Probably because what we will become through the waiting process is different. For me, waiting was about healing. For others, waiting may look like stepping out into new places. Whatever your waiting season looks like, here are three things I've learned through waiting that I want to share with you:

1. When Hope Seems Lost

Sometimes waiting can seem hopeless.

For me, writing was my dream. For you, maybe you've wanted to own your own business, create your own products, or go into a new field of work. Cling to that dream. Hold on to it.

There were days for me when my court cases seemed never-ending, or my abuser's attacks were fierce. I often felt lost and alone, but finding I wasn't alone made a big difference. Surrounding myself with other women who were ahead of me on the figurative road made a huge difference.

As I pursued my dream of writing, I had the opportunity to read books, listen to speakers, or learn from other people who talked about their journeys and how the waiting season of their journey was so valuable in the end. They say a person can live for a certain number of days without food and water, but not hope. I agree.

The biggest thing I can tell you is not to give up on yourself and your dreams. No matter how dire the situation is, there is still hope.

Stay strong. Your dream is unfolding, even if you can't see it. One of the first things I told a friend after I left my ex was that one day I wanted to write about my experiences, because I wanted other women to know they aren't alone. Living with intimate partner violence can feel very lonely because the abuser often pulls you away from your friends and family. To my readers who have experienced domestic violence or abuse: you are not alone! You have a story that one day you will share with others and give them hope as well. If you're in a season of waiting, it may seem hopeless, but I promise that when you look back, you will see the purpose in the wait.

2. Action in Waiting

Sometimes waiting can be long and boring.

I have this saying I often use. "Patience always pays off." Sometimes waiting is the last thing we want to do. Yet often waiting is the most important part, as the unseen steps are moving us closer to our dream.

As a teen, I was the bread-maker in the family. Since I had a large family, I'd make several loaves at once, letting them knead in our Bosch mixer. Unfortunately, someone had broken a lock-tab off the bowl that holds the lid on. Which meant I had to stand there for nearly ten minutes holding the lid on while the mixer kneaded the dough. I would huff, and sigh, and think of every other possible thing I could be doing while that dough was kneading.

Learning to wait patiently took a long time for me to master. Being comfortable with the uncomfortable, you might say, is one part of learning to wait. One of the best strategies I learned to utilize was working on other tasks while I waited. Whether that be at work or at home, if I were waiting on someone or something, I would find something to do while I was waiting.

In my writing, waiting meant letting my story formulate, as I learned to find my writing voice again. The more I wrote, the better writer I became. I surrounded myself with writing sources, following things on social media or online training programs that taught me new techniques, creating daily and weekly routines for my writing, and, especially, surrounding myself with people with similar goals to support me along the way.

Think about your dream. Maybe the timing isn't here yet, but are there things you can be doing that follow the same direction as your dream?

3. Trusting the Process

Sometimes we don't understand why we are waiting.

Looking back, throwing away that old manuscript may have been the first step to realizing how suppressed I was in my abusive marriage. While physical violence was terrifying, throwing away that hard work was the beginning of waking up to how bad things really were. Not just physically, but mentally and emotionally.

I see now how my writing needed to wait while I got myself and my child out of the unsafe situation we were in. I didn't see it at the time, but that figurative fire burning down my dreams was also the fire that drove me to get out. Do you ever feel like things are working against you, causing delays to your dreams and goals? But when you look back, you see how those delays were working things out on your behalf? I can see ways that God may have delayed my opportunities to write for my own safety and benefit. Are there actions you need to be taking right now that will ultimately move you closer to your own dream?

When the forest fire ends, new growth doesn't happen overnight. It takes time to rebuild.

Waiting is part of the process. It's not the pretty, glamorous, fun part. It's a long, sometimes lonely, grueling process. As you overcome the challenges and obstacles that stand in the way, you will start to see how the process of waiting is moving you closer to the dream you have.

When I first fled from my abusive marriage with my child, I had to take things one day at a time, one breath at a time. But as I worked through my separation, my healing journey, and rebuilding my life, even rebuilding myself, I was slowly able to look ahead. I was able to dream again. It was like building muscles; you may not see the results right away, but being consistent with your workout routine pays off. Waiting is like that. You may not see what's happening, but you still need to trust the process.

The Silenced Voice is the Loudest

My message is for the silenced writer. I believe you have a story to tell. I believe your experiences deserve to be shared. You are not alone. Hearing the stories of other women and survivors gave me the courage to face some of the hardest days because I knew I wasn't alone.

Standing up for yourself, your hopes, your dreams, can be scary, especially if you've been taught to keep peace and stay silent. Making myself and my dreams more of a priority felt odd after years of putting myself last.

Psalm 37:7 talks about not fretting when people carry out their wicked plans. Sometimes it felt like my abuser always had the upper hand. With renewed focus on my dreams and pressing forward through my healing, I learned to focus on my own goals and not worry about what he was doing, saying, or the ways he was lying to people around me. As I focused on myself and my child, rather than the chaos he was creating, I felt a shift inside of me. I started to see myself as more than a survivor, but rather, an overcomer, as I focused on helping others through their journeys, and focusing on my goals and dreams ahead.

Sometimes, it may seem like the door for you hasn't opened yet, but other people are walking through their own doors left and right. First, don't compare your story to someone else's. We each have our own stories, and we have our own journeys to make those things a reality. Let other people's stories inspire you rather than discourage you. Don't lose hope. Your door will open when the time is right. For me, once I was in a safer place, I started to see doors opening. I believe that your doors will open, too. Is there a shift you need to make right now that will ultimately move you closer to your dream and goals?

I believe we all have a dream deep inside of us. And if you're like me, it's not just one, but many dreams and goals. For me, writing and helping others to grow into a better version of themselves were important; for you, it may be something else. I believe you can make your goals and dreams a reality, one step at a time.

During the waiting seasons, things may seem hopeless, but don't give up. Continue to press forward, taking active steps while you wait. Trust the process of the waiting season.

You have a story to tell. Your voice will be heard. Your time will come.

Let Me Pray With You

Lord, Thank You for beautiful dreams. Show each person, each woman, each reader, the dreams You have for them. Surround her with those who will lift her up, instead of tearing her down. Keep her eyes forward, not worrying about those who want to rip her and her dreams down. Guide her through the wilderness of waiting, not to lose hope, or to grow weak, but to gain strength and clarity, and to press closer to You as she journeys forward. Thank You for giving us hope in the waiting. Amen (so be it).

About the Authors

Trisha K. Knight

Trisha K. Knight is a writer, missionary, decorator, poet, adventurer, and creative crafter. She enjoys traveling and learning new things. She loves animals, but especially loves her family and God. She spent her early years in the Pacific Northwest. She was a missionary in Germany for ten years, working with the hurting and lost. She returned to the States following the 2020 pandemic. Currently, she resides in the United States.

Email: tkknight@ymail.com

Sherrie Williams

Sherrie Williams is a homeschooling mama of six, fractional COO, and coach who helps people recognize patterns in their lives and steward their resources wisely. As a mother's ministry leader and consultant to women-led organizations, she creates elegant structures of depth, beauty, and simplicity that serve both families and vision. Through seasons of personal loss and transformation, she has learned to find hope in the waiting. She believes everything—from how we structure our days to how we spend our resources—is an opportunity to create something meaningful.

Website: www.sherrieanne.com/

Instagram: www.instagram.com/intentionalmotherhood

Sharri McGarry, M.A.

Sharri McGarry has a master's degree in clinical psychology with a graduate certificate in Addiction Studies. Her undergrad work included majors in Psychology and Family & Child Development, with a minor in Sociology/Criminology. She worked as an orthopaedic clinic specialist and served as Assistant to the Chief of Orthopaedics at a large hospital system while developing a psychology practice at New Life Clinics.

In 1993, Sharri underwent a life-saving experimental kidney/pancreas transplant, which allowed her to marry and have two sons. In 1998, she retired from her counseling practice and orthopaedic position to be a stay-at-home mom and homeschool her children.

Sharri is passionate about learning and about pointing people to Jesus Christ and healthy living through life and academic coaching.

Website: www.mcgarrycoaching.com

Facebook: www.facebook.com/sm.mcgarry93

www.facebook.com/profile.php?id=100036866665565

Linked In: www.linkedin.com/in/sharrimcgarry

www.linkedin.com/company/mcgarry-coaching-advising-for-life

Michelle L. Nelson

Michelle L. Nelson is the founder and content creator of *Our Words Have Power, LLC.*, a faith-based blog and social platform dedicated to encouraging others in their walk with God. She is also the author of the children's book *Little Ruby Does It Big*. A certified life coach and content specialist, Michelle previously served as a high school Reading, English, and Journalism teacher and Instructional Coach. She brings years of experience supporting children, youth, young adults, and families, helping people discover their identity in God and live with freedom, boldness, love, and purpose.

Website: www.OurWordsHavePower.com

Instagram: www.instagram.com/OurWordsHavePower

Linda J. Dingeldein

Linda J. Dingeldein, a pastor's wife who lives in rural Pennsylvania with her husband, Joel, uses the power of words and art to communicate her faith. With over thirty years of missionary experience, she is passionate about equipping women to live authentically in their God-given design. Linda is a fresh face in the writing world who has authored *Bella Bunny's Big Question: Grammy, Is Heaven For Real?* and *Praying Life in the Word: A Woman's Guide to Praying Scripture.* She inds joy in creating watercolor notecards and dreaming up stories with her two granddaughters, who endearingly call her "Crème Puff."

Website: www.lindajanedingeldein.com

Instagram: www.instagram.com/lindajanedingeldein

Facebook: www.facebook.com/LINDAJANEDINGELDEIN

Linda Berg

inda Berg** has lived a life centered on family, faith, and service. She married Brad, the love of her life, who, at the age of seven, told his mother he would one day marry her. Their marriage spanned 47 years, until April 2022, when Brad was called to his eternal home.

For twenty years, Linda dedicated herself to raising their seven children—six biological and one who joined their family by choice after leaving Happy Haven Children's Home. Together, Brad and Linda have 29 grandchildren, ranging from two months to 24 years old, and have created a cherished tradition of holding a "Grandparents' Camp" every other year to share life, faith, and God's Word with their family.

Linda's service extended beyond her home. While living in Mexico, she served as Office Manager at Rio Bravo Christian Ministries and as the Director of Women's and Children's Ministries. After retiring from that role, she and Brad worked as House Parents at Happy Haven Children's Home for girls in Cookeville, Tennessee, and following Brad's passing, Linda continued there as a case worker.

Her greatest confidence comes from her unwavering trust in God, who provides for her needs, guides her path, and grants comfort and peace through every season of life.

Kristy Howard

Kristy Howard is a mom of five, a chaplain, writer, and mentor for Christian women healing from shame-shaped religious systems. She serves alongside her husband in vocational ministry, and creates resources that help women rediscover identity in Christ, beauty and rest, and unshakable confidence through grace–not performance.

Website: www.kristyhowardwrites.com/

Facebook: www.facebook.com/kristyhowardwrites/

Instagram: www.instagram.com/kristyhowardwrites/

LinkedIn: www.linkedin.com/in/kristy-howard-writes/

Kim "Sparrow" Spencer

Kim "Sparrow" Spencer was born in Charleston, SC, to a single, unwed 17-year-old mom. After being in foster care, she was adopted and raised in Charlotte, NC. At the age of 17, she discovered, by accident, that her sister was her birth mother. She attributes her writing voice to this rocky set of circumstances, which shaped many of her attitudes about the world, and, more importantly, to the goodness of God, who blessed her for 43 years with a loving best friend for her husband and three amazing sons. She can say firsthand that God is with us in the waiting, and He has a good plan for our lives- a hope and a future. She resides in Charlotte with her dear sweetheart husband and their dog, Scout.

Julie Davis

$\mathcal{J}$ ulie Davis combines biblical wisdom with practical life lessons to encourage others to walk faithfully with God. She is passionate about equipping readers to live intentionally, stay grounded in truth, and pursue God's unique purpose for their lives. Julie and her husband live in Missouri, where they find joy in faith, family, and creating a legacy of hope and encouragement for those who come after them.

Instagram: www.instagram.com/juliedaviswrites

Amber Rose

*A*mber Rose holds a Bachelor of Arts in Communications and has completed specialized training in Writing for Children and Youth through the Institute for Children's Literature. From an early age, she's been driven by a pas-sion to become a published author and inspire others to overcome life's challenges and grow into the best version of themselves. In her free time, Amber enjoys painting, photography, and her newest hobby— practicing martial arts alongside family and friends.

Facebook: www.facebook.com/share/1AmX6yia5q/

Endnotes

Chapter 1

1. Maya Angelou. "fine art America" https://fineart america.com/featured/still-i-rise-maya-angelou-poem-vintage-paper-style-the-typography-tipi.html?gad_source=5&gad_campaignid=1510983999 Accessed 12 January 2026.

Chapter 2

1. Kampoy, Thierry. *Travail in Prayer: How Groanings in the Spirit Birth Revival, Healing, and Victory.* self-published, 2025. Page 8.

2. Medari, Victor Raj. "Dopamine, Desire, and Discipleship." *The Gospel Coalition*, 23 May 2025, in. thegospelcoalition.org/article/dopamine-desire-discipleship/.

3. Tripp, Paul David. *Journey to the Cross: A 40-Day Lenten Devotional.* Crossway, 2021. Page 26.

Chapter 3

1. *Donahue.* Created and hosted by Phil Donahue, Multimedia Entertainment, 1967–1996.

Chapter 5

1. Dingeldein, L. (2022) *Praying Life in the Word: A Woman's Guide to Praying Scripture.*

2. Ibed. pg. xxiii

Chapter 7

1. Rilke, Rainer Maria. *Letters to a Young Poet. Letter Four.* Translated by Stephen Mitchell, Penguin Classics, 2016.

Closing

Dear Reader,

Thank you for reading *Hope in the Waiting*!

I want to take a moment to celebrate the incredible authors who contributed to this meaningful book. They have poured their hearts into discovering, clarifying, and sharing their unique messages—and now, you get to benefit from their hard work and dedication.

At hope*books, we are deeply proud of our authors and are honored to partner with them on this journey. If you've ever considered writing and publishing your book, we invite you to visit hopebooks.com to learn more about our coaching and publishing services. We believe that everyone has a message to share and an audience to serve, and the world needs your hopeful words now more than ever.

Once again, let's take a moment to celebrate the hard work of these authors in bringing *Hope in the Waiting* to life.

Sincerely,

Brian Dixon

Publisher, hope*books

Looking to *connect* with a community of writers?

The world needs your *hope-filled* words more now than ever before.

Thinking about *writing* your own book?

hope*books
www.hopebooks.com